At Issue

Can Democracy Succeed in the Middle East?

Other books in the At Issue series:

At Issue

Can Democracy Succeed in the Middle East?

Jann Einfeld, Book Editor

GREENHAVEN PRESS

An imprint of Thomson Gale, a part of The Thomson Corporation

THOMSON

™

GALE

Detroit • New York • San Francisco • New Haven, Conn. • Waterville, Maine • London • Munich

THOMSON
————————✳———————— ™
GALE

Bonnie Szumski, *Publisher*
Helen Cothran, *Managing Editor*

© 2006 Thomson Gale, a part of The Thomson Corporation.

Thomson and Star logo are trademarks and Gale and Greenhaven Press are registered trademarks used herein under license.

For more information, contact:
Greenhaven Press
27500 Drake Rd.
Farmington Hills, MI 48331-3535
Or you can visit our Internet site at http://www.gale.com

LIBRARY OF CONGRESS CATALOGING-IN-PUBLICATION DATA

Can democracy succeed in the Middle East? / Jann Einfeld, book editor.
    p. cm. -- (At issue)
Includes bibliographical references and index.
ISBN 0-7377-3393-4 (lib. hardcover : alk. paper) -- ISBN 0-7377-3394-2 (pbk. : alk. paper)
    1. Democracy--Middle East. 2. Democratization--Middle East. 3. Middle East--Politics and government--1979- 4. United States--Foreign relations--Middle East. 5. Middle East--Foreign relations--United States. I. Einfeld, Jann. II. Title. III. Series.
    JQ1758.A91.C36 2006
    320.956--dc22

                                         2006021455

Printed in the United States of America
10 9 8 7 6 5 4 3 2 1

Contents

Introduction

> "The ball of liberty is now so well in mo-
> tion that it will roll around the globe. . . .
> Democracy's worldwide triumph is as-
> sured."
> —Thomas Jefferson,
> 1795

During the last decades of the twentieth century, tremendous optimism spread throughout the West that America's founding father Thomas Jefferson's vision of a democratic world was becoming a reality. Movements for democracy grew in the former Soviet Union as well as in many developing countries in corners of the globe long thought impervious to the influence of democracy. From 1974 to the end of the century, the percentage of the world's democratic nations doubled to 62 percent, or 120 of the 192 nations of the world. As the century drew to a close, however, the nations of the Middle East (with the exceptions of Israel and Turkey), and particularly Arab countries, remained resistant to any meaningful democratic reform.

Scholars, journalists, and foreign policy analysts disagree about why democracy has so far failed to take root in this part of the world. Some experts, like economic historian Charles Issawi, argue that democracy has not spread widely in the Middle East because many of the region's nations do not have a modern, industrialized economy, a middle class, and a literate population. Other commentators, such as U.S. policy adviser Jeanne Kirkpatrick, assert that the preconditions for democracy are not economic and social, but moral and cultural. They believe that Middle Eastern cultures and values do not support democracy. As Kirkpatrick writes, "It could take decades, if not centuries, for people to acquire the necessary disciplines and habits [that are congruent with democratic values]."

The debate over democracy in the Middle East took on a new momentum in the wake of the Islamic terrorist attack on the World Trade Center on September 11, 2001. The United States invaded Iraq, defeated Iraqi dictator Saddam Hussein, and proclaimed the promotion of democracy in Iraq and in the Middle East as its central weapon in the war on terrorism. Establishing democracies in the region, President George W. Bush contended, would bring stability to the volatile Middle East, the area of the world that poses the gravest threat to world peace. Implicit in this view was a rejection of the Kirkpatrick thesis, which had guided conservative foreign policy for decades. In November 2003, the president stated:

> In many nations of the Middle East, democracy has not yet taken root. And the questions arise: Are the people of the Middle East somehow beyond the reach of liberty? Are millions of men and women condemned by history and culture to live in despotism? Are they alone never to know freedom, and never even to have a choice in the matter? I, for one, do not believe it.

Bush rejects the argument that Middle Eastern cultures are incompatible with democracy, insisting to the contrary that democracy is the birthright and natural desire of every human being and would be readily embraced by the people of the Middle East. He backed a series of resolutions to promote democracy in Iraq and sent a bevy of officials to the Middle East to urge authoritarian leaders to implement democratic reforms.

In the first months of 2005 Bush's efforts helped trigger some significant developments hailed as evidence of a "democratic spring" in the region that had been dominated by autocrats for centuries: In Egypt, reforms were instituted to permit contested elections; in Saudi Arabia, the people voted in a municipal election, the first election of any kind conducted in the country; Syrian president Bashar Assad pledged to grant Syrian citizens the freedom to create new political parties; Lebanese citizens' protests accelerated the withdrawal of Syrian troops that had occupied Lebanon since 1990; and elections were held in Palestine. Finally, Iraq held its first democratic election in over thirty years, and representatives of two formerly repressed ethnic and religious groups took office (Kurd Jala Talabani became president and Shiite Ibrahim Jaafari was designated prime minister). In response to these developments, prominent Iraqi leader Humam Hamoudi notes, "People are beginning to feel their own authority, to feel they can create things for themselves, which is the beginning of democracy."

Optimism about the possibility of democracy taking hold in the Middle East waned, however, in late 2005 and 2006. This was due to a series of disheartening events, including the election of the radical Islamist group Hamas in the Palestine Authority; the election of representatives from the Islamic terrorist group Hizballah in Lebanon; sectarian violence in Iraq threatening civil war following the brutal and vicious attack by foreign insurgents on the Shiite Golden Mosque in Samarra; repression of opposition parties in Egypt; and Syria's continued presence in Lebanon and resistance to democratic reforms. "Despite its auspicious beginnings," writes political scientist Steven Heydemann,

> the past year [2005] did not produce a turning point in the struggle for political change in the Arab world. Instead, the evident limits of the "Arab spring" have reinforced the depressing pattern of half-step forward, half-step back that has defined the pace of democratization in the region for at least two decades.

Unfolding events in the Middle East continue to challenge Jefferson's assertion of the eventual worldwide triumph of democracy. It remains unclear whether democracy will succeed in this part of the world that has resisted it for so long. What is clear, however, is that democracy's progress in the Middle East will be neither swift nor predictable, and that spreading democracy in this part of the world will require the enormous determination of its champions. In *At Issue: Can Democracy Succeed in the Middle East?* the authors offer a variety of perspectives on the debate over the future of democracy in the Middle East. Leading experts, scholars, and policy makers also debate whether Islam and democracy are compatible, whether Arabs and Muslims actually want democracy; and whether expanding the rights of Middle Eastern women is a prerequisite for the spread of democracy in this region. Given its implications for world peace and the safety of world citizenry, this debate is one of the foremost foreign policy concerns of the twenty-first century.

1

Democracy Can Succeed in the Middle East

Condoleezza Rice

A former political scientist at Stanford University, Condoleezza Rice was sworn in as U.S. secretary of state in January 2005. Prior to that appointment, Rice had served as the national security adviser to President George W. Bush since 2001.

Throughout the Middle East, people are losing patience with repressive regimes and are demanding freedom and democracy. The citizens of Iraq, Lebanon, Syria, Iran, and other Middle Eastern countries are courageously seeking democratic reforms. Democracy is the system that protects the rights that all human beings deserve—the right to live without fear, to speak freely, and to practice the religion of their choice. The United States and the free world support the democratic aspirations of the people of the Middle East, who will achieve their dreams for liberty and democracy.

Editor's note: The following selection is an extract of a speech Condoleezza Rice delivered at the American University in Cairo, Egypt, in 2005.

In our world today, a growing number of men and women are securing their liberty. And as these people gain the power to choose, they are creating democratic governments in order to protect their natural rights.

We should all look to a future when every government respects the will of its citizens—because the ideal of democracy

Condoleezza Rice, "Remarks at the American University in Cairo," Cairo, Egypt, July 20, 2005. U.S. Department of State, www.state.gov.

is universal. For 60 years, my country, the United States, pursued stability at the expense of democracy in this region here in the Middle East—and we achieved neither. Now, we are taking a different course. We are supporting the democratic aspirations of all people.

As President [George W.] Bush said in his Second Inaugural Address [on January 20, 2005]: "America will not impose our style of government on the unwilling. Our goal instead is to help others find their own voice, to attain their own freedom, and to make their own way."

Here in the Middle East . . . millions of people are demanding freedom for themselves and democracy for their countries.

We know these advances will not come easily, or all at once. We know that different societies will find forms of democracy that work for them. When we talk about democracy, though, we are referring to governments that protect certain basic rights for all their citizens—among these, the right to speak freely. The right to associate. The right to worship as you wish. The freedom to educate your children—boys and girls. And freedom from the midnight knock of the secret police.

Securing these rights is the hope of every citizen, and the duty of every government. In my own country, the progress of democracy has been long and difficult. And given our history, the United States has no cause for false pride and we have every reason for humility.

After all, America was founded by individuals who knew that all human beings—and the governments they create—are inherently imperfect. And the United States was born half free and half slave. And it was only in my lifetime that my government guaranteed the right to vote for all of its people.

Nevertheless, the principles enshrined in our Constitution enable citizens of conviction to move America closer every day to the ideal of democracy. Here in the Middle East, that same long hopeful process of democratic change is now beginning to unfold. Millions of people are demanding freedom for themselves and democracy for their countries.

In Iraq, millions of people are refusing to surrender to terror the dream of freedom and democracy.

Democratic Reforms in the Middle East

To these courageous men and women, I say today: All free nations will stand with you as you secure the blessings of your own liberty. I have just come from Jordan, where I met with the King and Queen—two leaders who have embraced reform for many years. And Jordan's education reforms are an example for the entire region. That government is moving toward political reforms that will decentralize power and give Jordanians a greater stake in their future.

In Iraq, millions of citizens are refusing to surrender to terror the dream of freedom and democracy. When Baghdad was first designed, over twelve-hundred years ago, it was conceived as the "Round City"—a city in which no citizen would be closer to the center of justice than any other. Today—after decades of murder, and tyranny, and injustice—the citizens of Iraq are again reaching for the ideals of the Round City.

Despite the attacks of violent and evil men, ordinary Iraqis are displaying great personal courage and remarkable resolve. And every step of the way—from regaining their sovereignty, to holding elections, to . . . writing a constitution—the people of Iraq are exceeding all expectations.

The Palestinian people have also spoken. And their freely elected government is working to seize the best opportunity in years to fulfill their historic dream of statehood. Courageous leaders, both among the Palestinians and the Israelis, are dedicated to seeking that peace. And they are working to build a shared trust.

The Palestinian Authority will soon take control of the Gaza—a first step toward realizing the vision of two democratic states living side by side in peace and security. As Palestinians fight terror, and as the Israelis fulfill their obligations and responsibilities to help create a viable Palestinian state, the entire world—especially Egypt and the United States—will offer full support.

In Lebanon, supporters of democracy are demanding independence from foreign masters. After the assassination of [former prime minister] Rafiq Hariri, thousands of Lebanese citizens called for change. And when the murder of journalist Samir Qaseer reminded everyone of the reach and brutality of terror, the Lebanese people were still unafraid.

They mourned their fellow patriot, but they united publicly with pens and pencils held aloft. It is not only the Lebanese people who desire freedom from Syria's police state. The Syrian people themselves share that aspiration.

One hundred and seventy-nine Syrian academics and human rights activists are calling upon their government to "let the Damascus spring flower, and let its flowers bloom." Syria's leaders should embrace this call—and learn to trust their people. The case of Syria is especially serious, because as its neighbors embrace democracy and political reform, Syria continues to harbor or directly support groups committed to violence—in Lebanon, and in Israel, and Iraq, and in the Palestinian territories. It is time for Syria to make a strategic choice to join the progress that is going on all around it.

Opposition to Oppressive Regimes

In Iran, people are losing patience with an oppressive regime that denies them their liberty and their rights. The appearance of elections does not mask the organized cruelty of Iran's theocratic state. The Iranian people . . . are capable of liberty. They desire liberty. And they deserve liberty. The time has come for the unelected few to release their grip on the aspirations of the proud people of Iran.

In Saudi Arabia, brave citizens are demanding accountable government. And some good first steps toward openness have been taken with recent municipal elections. Yet many people pay an unfair price for exercising their basic rights. Three individuals in particular are currently imprisoned for peacefully petitioning their government. That should not be a crime in any country.

Now, here in Cairo, President [Hosni] Mubarak's decision to amend the country's constitution and hold multiparty elections is encouraging. President Mubarak has unlocked the door for change. Now, the Egyptian Government must put its faith in its own people. We are all concerned for the future of Egypt's reforms when peaceful supporters of democracy— men and women—are not free from violence. The day must come when the rule of law replaces emergency decrees—and when the independent judiciary replaces arbitrary justice.

The Egyptian Government must fulfill the promise it has made to its people—and to the entire world—by giving its citizens the freedom to choose. Egypt's elections, including the Parliamentary elections, must meet objective standards that define every free election.

Successful (democratic) reform is always homegrown.

Opposition groups must be free to assemble, and to participate, and to speak to the media. Voting should occur without violence or intimidation. And international election monitors and observers must have unrestricted access to do their jobs.

Those who would participate in elections, both supporters and opponents of the government, also have responsibilities.

They must accept the rule of law, they must reject violence, they must respect the standards of free elections, and they must peacefully accept the results.

The Truth About Democracy

Throughout the Middle East, the fear of free choices can no longer justify the denial of liberty. It is time to abandon the excuses that are made to avoid the hard work of democracy. There are those who say that democracy is being imposed. In fact, the opposite is true: Democracy is never imposed. It is tyranny that must be imposed.

People choose democracy freely. And successful reform is always homegrown. Just look around the world today. For the first time in history, more people are citizens of democracies than of any other form of government. This is the result of choice, not of coercion.

There are those who say that democracy leads to chaos, or conflict, or terror. In fact, the opposite is true: Freedom and democracy are the only ideas powerful enough to overcome hatred, and division, and violence. For people of diverse races and religions, the inclusive nature of democracy can lift the fear of difference that some believe is a license to kill. But people of goodwill must choose to embrace the challenge of listening, and debating, and cooperating with one another.

For neighboring countries with turbulent histories, democracy can help to build trust and settle old disputes with dignity. But leaders of vision and character must commit themselves to the difficult work that nurtures the hope of peace. And for all citizens with grievances, democracy can be a path to lasting justice. But the democratic system cannot function if certain groups have one foot in the realm of politics and one foot in the camp of terror.

The Importance of Freedom

There are those who say that democracy destroys social institutions and erodes moral standards. In fact, the opposite is true: The success of democracy depends on public character and private virtue. For democracy to thrive, free citizens must work every day to strengthen their families, to care for their neighbors, and to support their communities.

Across the Middle East today, millions of citizens are voicing their aspirations for liberty and for democracy.

There are those who say that long-term economic and social progress can be achieved without free minds and free markets. In fact, human potential and creativity are only fully released when governments trust their people's decisions and invest in their people's future. And the key investment is in those people's education. Because education—for men and for women—transforms their dreams into reality and enables them to overcome poverty.

There are those who say that democracy is for men alone. In fact, the opposite is true: Half a democracy is not a democracy. As one Muslim woman leader has said, "Society is like a bird. It has two wings. And a bird cannot fly if one wing is broken." Across the Middle East, women are inspiring us all.

In Kuwait, women protested to win their right to vote, carrying signs that declared: "Women are Kuwaitis, too." [In June 2005], Kuwait's legislature voiced its agreement. In Saudi Arabia, the promise of dignity is awakening in some young women. During the recent municipal elections, I saw the image of a father who went to vote with his daughter.

Rather than cast his vote himself, he gave the ballot to his daughter, and she placed it in the ballot box. This small act of hope reveals one man's dream for his daughter. And he is not alone. . . .

Democracy is the Ideal Path

Across the Middle East today, millions of citizens are voicing their aspirations for liberty and for democracy. These men

17

and women are expanding boundaries in ways many thought impossible just one year ago [in 2004].

They are demonstrating that all great moral achievements begin with individuals who do not accept that the reality of today must also be the reality of tomorrow.

There was a time, not long ago, after all, when liberty was threatened by slavery.

A hopeful future is within reach ... of every man and woman in the Middle East.

The moral worth of my ancestors, it was thought, should be valued by the demand of the market, not by the dignity of their souls. This practice was sustained through violence. But the crime of human slavery could not withstand the power of human liberty. What seemed impossible in one century became inevitable in the next.

There was a time, even more recently, when liberty was threatened by colonialism. It was believed that certain peoples required foreign masters to rule their lands and run their lives. Like slavery, this ideology of injustice was enforced through oppression.

But when brave people demanded their rights, the truth that freedom is the destiny of every nation rang true throughout the world. What seemed impossible in one decade became inevitable in the next.

Today, liberty is threatened by undemocratic governments. Some believe this is a permanent fact of history. But there are others who know better. These impatient patriots can be found in Baghdad and Beirut, in Riyadh and in Ramallah, in Amman and in Tehran and right here in Cairo.

Together, they are defining a new standard of justice for our time—a standard that is clear, and powerful, and inspiring: Liberty is the universal longing of every soul, and democracy is the ideal path for every nation.

The day is coming when the promise of a fully free and democratic world, once thought impossible, will also seem inevitable. . . .

A hopeful future is within the reach of every Egyptian citizen—and every man and woman in the Middle East.

2

Democracy Cannot Succeed in the Middle East

Michael Stent

Prior to his current position as Middle East correspondent for South Africa's Cape Times, *veteran journalist Michael Stent was managing editor of the* Gulf News *in Dubai, the United Arab Emirates.*

Although President George W. Bush, U.S. Secretary of State Condoleezza Rice, and others assert that democratic reform in the Middle East is highly desirable and a prerequisite for world peace, there is little evidence that any meaningful reform is underway in the region. Those who lead the reform movement are conservative Islamists who will not implement any meaningful reform, and, furthermore, most Middle Easterners have no desire for democracy. With no real support for democratic reform from within the Middle East, the prospects for democracy and world peace are bleak.

The problem with conventional wisdom is that it is seldom wise and almost invariably false. Since [the terrorist attacks of] 9/11 [2001] cast the world into a new cold (and, in places, very hot) war, it has become accepted that a prerequisite for international stability is reform in the Middle East.

[U.S. secretary of state] Condoleezza Rice says so, [U.S. president] George W. Bush insists upon it, so does [UK prime minister] Tony Blair, and [average citizens] Thomas, Richard and Harry all agree.

They might well be right, but then don't hold your breath waiting for the world to become a more stable place. It won't happen because the Middle East has reformed in the image of the West. Hosni Mubarak's election—if one can dignify the process with that word—for a fifth six-year term as president of Egypt forcefully underlies that.

There are many worthy strands to the reform argument. Democracy is self-evidently a good thing and all Middle Eastern nations are, in one form or another, totalitarian. There are the absolute monarchies—Saudi Arabia, Jordan, Kuwait, Bahrain, Qatar, the United Arab Emirates, Oman—and the one-party states, Egypt and Syria.

Lebanon has some democratic characteristics, although the Syrian withdrawal after the assassination of former prime minister Rafik Hariri has led to a reversion to the sectarian politics that preceded the country's ruinous civil war.

Leave aside Iraq and Israel-Palestine for the time being, because they are not in the reforming claque's sights. The pro-reformists are right. An open society is, well, simply a good and desirable thing for most concerned.

Democracy, good sense and a preference to avoid violence are thoroughly desirable—but it makes not a jot of difference to reality.

Democracy Is Needed but Unlikely

Totalitarian states are also intrinsically troubling. The present incumbents in the Middle East might be good pro-Western chaps (with the exception of Syria), but there is no telling what they might become or how their successors will behave.

Critical to this concern is oil. Nepal is an absolute monarchy and as totalitarian as it gets. The king is a dangerous and unstable man. But Nepal has little to commend it, other than the Himalayas, and is therefore not worth much international concern.

As the world's largest oil-exporting region, the Middle East cannot be arbitrarily ruled. Decisions need to be sensible and serve international stability. Democracy, the reformists would say and probably quite correctly, produces the best decisions, in the long run at least.

The advocates of reform also argue that democracy would stifle extremism—the Islamic fundamentalism that has become their new communism. Again, they might be right. Societies shrouded in secrecy and repression are breeding grounds for extreme views and will swell the ranks of al-Qaeda [terrorist group] and its ilk.

All this might well be true—democracy, good sense and a preference to avoid violence are thoroughly desirable—but it makes not a jot of difference to reality.

Even Reformers Adhere to Islam

What the Western pro-change group seems to fail to realise is that its concept of reform and that of reformists in the Middle East are far removed from each other.

If there is change away from theocratic monarchy or the more secular dictatorships of Syria and Egypt, it will almost certainly not be to the West's tastes.

The election of Mahmoud Ahmedinejad as president of Iran . . . underlines that point. He, a populist, defeated [former president] Akbar Hashemi Rafsanjani, a powerful member of the establishment, by a comprehensive margin. Ahmedinejad was able to mobilise the support of the poor and unemployed. He touched a nerve and swept the election.

Both men, though, are religious conservatives. That is, and will be for some time, a requirement for political power in most Middle Eastern countries. Politics and theology will be inseparable.

This is not surprising. The European [Protestant] Reformation was thus. And currently, American politics is in the thrall of Christian fundamentalism and its neo-con[servative] political and social outgrowths.

Reform based on a firm adherence to Islam—and probably a conservative version of it—will be deeply uncomfortable for the West, however democratic the process of change might be.

This is obvious in the case of Egypt.

On her visit there [in early 2005], Rice had a great deal to say about reform and democracy. Egypt, as a close ally and the beneficiary of considerable sums of US aid, might well have listened.

Mubarak simply ignored her and went ahead with the farcical poll that saw his support tumble from the statutory 99% to 88%.

The real opposition in Egypt was not on show. It is banned from participating in politics and suffers under a heavy government hand. It is the Muslim Brotherhood [Islamic fundamentalists], an important part of Egypt's emergence as a modern state, then promptly banned by the politicians more than 50 years ago.

The Brotherhood, and allied movements such as the Kefayah (Enough) protesters [who protest Mubarak and U.S. Middle East policies], could possibly command majority support in Egypt, although obviously there is no way to test that now. They—like [Islamic extremist group] Hamas in Palestine—are popular with the poor, whom they serve through schools and other social welfare programmes.

They are part of the community, unlike the distant politicians who rule.

If the Brotherhood came to power, however proper the processes were, it would be profoundly uncomfortable for the US and its Western allies. The same would be true if a similar movement overthrew one of the monarchies, or took power in Iraq or Syria.

U.S. Support for Israel Stymies Reform

There is a simple reason for this: the US is totally committed to the preservation and security of a Jewish state of Israel. A secular unitary state or, heaven forfend, a unitary Islamic Palestine incorporating Israel is simply not on the agenda.

Israel is arguably the only consistent and enduring element of American foreign policy. The US will not, under any circumstances, compromise this.

Support for Israel is probably even more fervent under the George W. Bush administration than it was previously because of the odd fundamentalist theology that demands the existence of a political state of Israel before the Second Coming [of Christ] can occur.

This stymies reforms as they might happen naturally within Middle Eastern countries. Whatever the talk, the results of change must be consistent with the Israeli policy of the US.

Thus, Mubarak has been a stalwart ally on Israel. He has delivered on most of his promises to keep Israel secure. Whatever his numerous democratic deficits, he is a man with whom the US is used to dealing and will happily continue trading.

It is . . . questionable as to whether there is much concerted appetite for reform among the nationals of [most] Middle Eastern countries.

The same would apply to the monarchies. All have, over the past two decades at least, not interfered with Israel's steady expansion into Palestinian territories and its refusal to explore viable solutions to the conflict.

The rulers do make the occasional critical statement, of course, and overtly shun relations with Israel, but this is window-dressing. They have most lucrative trade and financial relations with the West and host large US military bases. Most were educated in the US or Britain and have fond memories and close contacts there.

They will certainly not let the small matter of Palestine upset that apple cart.

No Real Appetite for Reform

There will, of course, be some tinkering on the margins of society. The West is increasingly entering into free trade agreements (FTAs) with the [Persian] Gulf countries, in particular. These require conformity to certain standards, such as allowing trade unions. So, unions will be formed, but they will be so tightly circumscribed as to be powerless.

It is also questionable whether there is much concerted appetite for reform among the nationals of all Middle Eastern countries except Egypt, Lebanon and possibly Syria. And for reform to endure and prosper, it must come from within.

The Gulf states all have very large expatriate populations which are, and will continue to be, entirely excluded from the political process. Such domestic demands for change—polite requests would be a more accurate term—have little meat to them. In Saudi Arabia, for example, the pressing issue recently before the appointed consultative council was whether even to discuss whether women should be allowed to drive. They decided against the debate.

With little impetus for democratic reform within most countries, . . . the prospects for change in the Middle East are slight.

The largely prosperous nationals have an enviable lifestyle and they will be unlikely to want to rock the boat too much. One direction, though, might be towards greater religiosity in the face of the swarming crowds of foreigners who, demographically, swamp them.

Saudi Arabia has a few pockets of dissidence, but the authorities deal swiftly and emphatically with these. Apart from that, not too much at all.

No Reform and No Peace

So, with little impetus for democratic reform within most countries, and "undesirable elements" leading the reform movement in a couple, the prospects for change in the Middle East are slight.

Imposed "regime change" appears to apply only to Iraq—hardly an eloquent advertisement for the benefits of democracy—and possibly Syria.

The central problem of Israel-Palestine will not be addressed in any way that renders it open to long-term solutions.

So the world—persuaded that Middle Eastern reform and international peace are inseparable—will be disappointed.

There will be no reform and there will be no peace. The new grand conflict has begun and . . . will probably long outlast most of us.

Christian fundamentalism, Islamic fundamentalism and Jewish fundamentalism will continue to bash heads. Islamic extremists will not be happy until Israel and its Jewish inhabitants are obliterated and all Western infidel troops leave Muslim lands. For as long as Israel is under threat, Western troops certainly will not leave.

Jewish extremists, meanwhile, will continue to use the excuse of Islamic extremism to refuse to settle with the overwhelmingly sensible Muslim majority and will thus play into the extremists' hands.

Christian fundamentalists will continue to favour Israel over all other claimants to their attention. Again, extremism will profit.

It is a bleak prospect, and many people will continue to be killed and injured throughout the world. There will be no reform and there will be no peace. The new grand conflict has begun and, like the Cold War, will probably long outlast most of us.

3

The United States Can Bring Democracy to the Middle East

Karl Zinsmeister

Karl Zinsmeister is the editor in chief of the American Enterprise, *the monthly journal of the American Enterprise Institute for Public Policy Research in Washington, D.C. His recent published works include* Boots on the Ground: A Month with the 82nd Airborne in the Battle for Iraq *(2003) and* Dawn over Baghdad: How the U.S. Military Is Using Bullets and Ballots to Remake Iraq *(2004).*

Many liberals and some conservatives who opposed President George W. Bush's aggressive efforts to bring democracy to the Middle East now acknowledge they were wrong. Fears about the triumph of religious extremists in Iraq have proved unfounded. Most Iraqis have welcomed the U.S. liberation of their country and have shown they are ready to implement democracy. As in most places where democracy has triumphed, superior military strength was the source of this victory. The determination of President Bush, backed by the military prowess of the U.S. armed forces, has created a turning point in world history by bringing political freedom to the Middle East for the first time in ten thousand years.

> "Arabs are marching for freedom and shouting slogans against tyrants in the streets of Beirut and Cairo—and regimes that have endured for decades are visibly tottering. Those who claimed that U.S. intervention could never produce such events have reason to reconsider."
>
> —Washington Post *column by Jackson Diehl*

Karl Zinsmeister, "In the Middle East, A New World," *American Enterprise*, vol. 16, April/May 2005, pp. 4–8. Copyright 2005, American Enterprise Institute for Public Policy Research. Reproduced with permission of The American Enterprise.

Those of us who spent much of 2003 and 2004 urging Americans not to give up on Iraq can attest that those two years were stained with many harsh attacks, much niggling criticism, and abundant disdain for America's aggressive efforts to reshape the dysfunctional governments of the Middle East into more humane and peaceful forms. From the very beginning, of course, the [George W.] Bush administration's left-wing enemies in the U.S. and Europe were hysterically opposed to the push for Middle Eastern democracy. A significant number of right-wing pundits also proved themselves to be sunshine patriots of the worst sort—bailing out of the hard, dirty work of war and cultural transformation as soon as the predictable resistance arose.

America's venture to defang the Middle East is neither ... [a] selfish oil grab ... nor a dreamy and doomed Don Quixote crusade.

But that's politics. In Washington, if you're looking for a brave and steadfast ally, you need to buy a dog. Fortunately our warriors battling away in [the Iraqi cities of] Najaf and Samarra and Anbar province didn't surrender to the Beltway [District of Columbia] gloom that defeated most of our media and political elites.

Everyday Americans also proved sturdier than our chattering class. They stayed with the fight long enough for some hard facts to emerge. Now some very good news is obvious to all who have eyes: We are *not* facing a popular revolt in Iraq. Average Arabs are *not* on the side of terrorists and Islamic radicals. America's venture to defang the Middle East is neither the cynical and selfish oil grab that the lunatic Left have claimed, nor a dreamy and doomed Don Quixote crusade as some conservative grumps insisted.

So here, at last, come the soldiers of the "me too" brigade. Even the French have joined in. They're sending one man (yes, one) to help train Iraqi security forces. And he's welcome. Victory is magnanimous.

Liberty Creates Peace

I do not (as those of you who have read my books about the war know) claim that happy days are here again, that the future will bring nothing but a cheery whirl of American marshmallow roasts with the lovely people of the Middle East. For my entire lifetime, this has been the worst-governed part of the planet. Its economic policies are in a photo finish with Africa's as the globe's most counterproductive. Ignorance and illiteracy are widespread, and Middle Easterners nurse more superstitions, blood feuds, and ugly prejudices than any people I have ever traveled and worked among.

But that's exactly why America finally plunged in to help drain this swamp and plant seeds for a healthier future. The paralyzing error of "don't rock the boat" types like [former U.S. national security advisers] Brent Scowcroft [and] Zbigniew Brzezinski, [conservative commentator] Pat Buchananan, [former national security adviser] Richard Clarke, and others who attacked the Iraq war as overambitious is the assumption that political and economic freedom can be brought to the Middle East only after it is already full of Rotary clubs and Wal-Marts. Note to so-called "realists": You've got your causation all backwards. It is liberty that creates peace, stability, and decency in a nation—not the reverse. If you wait until a country is serene and prosperous before introducing political and economic freedom, you will wait forever.

Obstacles to Democracy

Many daunting obstacles still lay ahead in the Middle East. [Conservative commentator] Steven Vincent warns how important it is that moderates in the Muslim world wrest control of their religion from the extremists who presently have far too much influence. In a chapter called "The Character

Test" and elsewhere in *Dawn over Baghdad*, I discuss some of the cultural baggage that Middle Easterners need to discard as they become self-ruling: pervasive dishonesty and graft, a shortage of altruism, destructive paranoia, widespread passivity and sloth, a weak ethic of personal responsibility, an attraction to strongmen.

[Lebanese politician] Walid Jumblatt . . . has periodically made nasty cracks about the U.S., Jews, and Western mores. When an Iraqi hotel was rocketed . . . while U.S. Undersecretary of Defense Paul Wolfowitz was sleeping in it, Jumblatt remarked that it was too bad Wolfowitz escaped. This is not a man most Americans would want their daughter to marry. But that's not the right test. A new generation of elected Middle Eastern leaders doesn't have to love us. We can be thrilled that they will simply leave us alone, and (by treating their own people better than today's despots) stop turning out young men so homicidally frustrated with their lot in life as to become killers.

Democracy As Antidote to Extremism

America's struggle with incivility from the Middle East will continue in the years ahead, and we will have to hold our noses at times as the various countries in the region make their way from fascistic to freely elected governance. In Lebanon, for instance, even after the Syrian thugocracy is ejected, the country will have to figure out how to assimilate into a peaceful national politics the substantial minority of Lebanese who support the atrocious locally based terrorist group Hezbollah.

Nearly every Muslim country has a potentially troublesome extremist minority; in some of them it is big enough to influence the government. Even Turkey, traditionally one of the most moderate Islamic nations, is currently run by a party that throws around ludicrous allegations that the U.S. harvests Iraqi organs for sale back home, is secretly injecting Christianity and Judaism into Muslim countries, and so forth. Turkish Prime Minister [Recep Tayyip] Erdogan tried to paint the January [2006] balloting in Iraq as illegitimate, until the Iraqis themselves put the lie to that.

But these sorts of shrieks and shouts are how democracies blow off steam and gradually fold discontented factions into national compromises. Demagogic politicians, newspaper lies, and popular conspiracy theories are part and parcel of life in every nation with free politics. Ever heard of Al Sharpton?[1] Over the long run, I'll say again, participatory government works as an *antidote* to political extremism, not an enabler.

It can no longer be denied that the vast majority of Iraqis oppose the terrorists.

No Islamic Theocracy

I'll never forget the day I received the results of Iraq's first scientific national opinion poll, which we at *The American Enterprise* wrote and conducted in August 2003. Beneath the noise and bluster typical of Middle Eastern politics, I could see in the data the outlines of a large silent majority in Iraq that is much more sensible than one would guess from media portrayals. In a September [2003] news conference where we released the findings, we pointed out that two thirds of Iraqis did not want an Islamic theocracy, that three quarters of the public wanted [Iraqi dictator Saddam Hussein's] Baathist cronies punished, that Iraqi opinion of [Islamic terrorist leader] Osama bin Laden was far more negative than positive, that Iraqis' favorite model for a new government was the U.S.

In a chapter of *Dawn over Baghdad* titled "What Ordinary Iraqis Want," including subsections "No Need for Nightmares," "The Un-Fanatics," and "Unpopular Insurgents," I reiterated many of these points, and added observations (drawn from

---

1. The Reverend Al Sharpton is a Pentecostal minister, civil rights activist and celebrity personality. He ran for the Democratic Party nomination for president in 2004.

my time spent in Iraq's Shiite southern half) on the relative moderation of Iraq's majority Shias. Over the past year, AEI [American Enterprise Institute] Islamic expert Reuel Gerecht has made many similar points. . . . Alas, non-dire views like these were mostly ignored or discounted during the feeding frenzy of media negativity and defeatism that took hold shortly after the liberation of Baghdad and dominated Iraq reporting right up until the January [2005] election.

Thankfully, the election finally exposed the falsity of claims that Iraqis were unwilling participants in America's liberation of their country. It can no longer be denied that the vast majority of Iraqis oppose the terrorists. Our Eeyores[2] have now shifted their worries, however, to the idea that Iraqis are likely to repeat the Iranian nightmare and veer into mullah-ridden theocracy.

Clearly a critical mass of Iraqis are ready to experiment with political tolerance and pluralism for the first time ever.

Iraq Embraces Political Pluralism

Not likely. It isn't just that Iraqis have the benefit of knowing what a mess the clerics produced in Iran. It isn't just that Iraq's Kurds would put the brakes on any such attempt. It isn't just the repeated assurances by leading Shiites that they have no intention of imposing Islamic law on the country, and want to encompass all of Iraq's many peoples in the government they will lead. What is perhaps most soothing is seeing who exactly the Shiites are pushing forth as their representatives. The parliamentarians backed by Ayatollah Sistani include many Western-educated professionals, scientists, representatives of all ethnic and religious groups, and diverse points

---

2. Eeyore is a character from the Winnie-the-Pooh stories who is always worried and gloomy.

of view, even former communists and ex-monarchists. Most strikingly, one out of every three nominees is female—an utterly un-Khomeini-ish statement.

The man asked by Sistani to recruit election candidates, Hussein Shahrestani, is a nuclear physicist—hardly someone at cross purposes with modernity. After being tortured by [former Iraqi leader] Saddam [Hussein], he escaped to Iran, where he was sufficiently put off by the ruling clergy that he fled again to Britain. He may not exactly be a NASCAR [National Association for Stock Car Auto Racing] dad, but this is the kind of Iraqi Americans can work with, and live next to.

The forbearance that Iraq's Shiites have demonstrated over the last year strikes me as heroically impressive. Despite scores of horrible provocations—terrorists blasting weddings, shrines, beloved leaders, all in the hope of inciting a backlash that might spark an Iraqi civil war—the Shia have refused to retaliate or match tit for tat (as the longstanding Arab tradition of vengeance calls for). Clearly, a critical mass of Iraqis are ready to experiment with political tolerance and pluralism for the first time ever.

Keep Western Expectations Modest

While a replay of the [1979 Iranian revolutionary leader and fundamentalist Muslim Ayatollah] Khomeini nightmare seems dubious, we should keep our expectations modest when it comes to the newly emerging politics of the Arab world. In particular, we need to give Iraq's Shiites room to be Shiites. Many of the people the Iraqis choose as their leaders will not look or sound like Western politicians. The constitution they will draft . . . is not likely to be one that Americans would want to live under. Some new Iraqi laws will make us squeamish. All this we must accept.

Introducing democracy does not mean that other people must remake themselves in our image. Beyond respecting basic human dignities, Iraqis should have the right to shape their society as they see best—including basing it on traditional Islamic precepts if they choose. We in the West must not anathematize Islamic law; our goal should instead be to housebreak Islamic fundamentalism, to link it to democratic due process so that the potential for tyrannizing and bellicosity is tamed out of it.

The first Islamic democracies are not likely to be places where we would be tempted to take our kids for vacation. Even the friendliest ones will sometimes be rhetorically quite anti-American. Then again, so is France. We don't need affection from Middle Easterners; we need only peace.

We have brought political freedom to places that had never tasted such in 10,000 years of local history.

Besides, there are plenty of social questions where modern Western solutions may not necessarily be the best ones. If Islamic nations choose to ban pornography, if they want a different balance between work and leisure, if they prefer their own patterns of family life, Americans should be perfectly satisfied to let them follow an alternate path. . . .

U.S. Military Brings Hope to Middle East

In general, however, the U.S. can be very proud of the "cultural imperialism" it has practiced in the Middle East over the last three years. We have brought political freedom to places that had never tasted such in 10,000 years of local history. "It is outrageous and amazing that the first free and general elections in the history of the Arab nation are to take place in Iraq, under the auspices of the American occupation, and in Palestine, under the auspices of the Israeli occupation," commented [Jordanian activist] Salameh Nematt in the Arabic daily *Dar al-Hayat*.

Of course the elections in Afghanistan and Iraq, and all that has followed in Palestine, Lebanon, Egypt, Saudi Arabia, and elsewhere, didn't just happen. They required enormous acts of American will. Anyone who thinks these breakthroughs would have occurred under a Commander in Chief less bold and stubborn than George W. Bush is mad.

The fresh hope now pulsing through the Middle East is not the result of diplomacy, or U.N. [United Nations] programs, or foreign aid, or expanded trade, or carrots offered by Europeans or multilateral negotiations, or visits from [actor/activist] Sean Penn. It is the fruit of fierce U.S. military strength, real toughness on the part of the middle American public, and a tremendous hardness in the person of our President and his staff.

As I write this, amidst a beautiful March blizzard, I am gulping tea from a mug emblazoned with the shield of one of the U.S. military units I spent time with in Iraq, the 1st Battalion of the 5th Marines. Their motto reads: "MAKE PEACE, OR DIE." Since 9/11, that is exactly the offer we've extended to thousands of terrorists and a handful of governments. And it has worked. Sometimes America's message needs to be just that simple.

Bush Deserves Credit

Luckily, our country had a leader willing to communicate this clearly, and the steeliness to shoulder the losses that come with any righteous war, exactly when we needed him. There were a thousand points where the democracy train now pulling into the Middle East could have gone off the tracks. The only reason we made it through the handwringing of 2003 and 2004 was because the engineer had nerve.

This is finally being acknowledged even by George Bush's enemies: "The Bush administration is entitled to claim a healthy share of the credit for many of these advances. It boldly proclaimed the cause of Middle East democracy at a time when few in the West thought it had any realistic chance," conceded the *New York Times* on March 1, 2005, with the concluding understatement that "there could have been no democratic elections in Iraq this January if Saddam Hussein had still been in power."

That same week, *Der Spiegel*, the German weekly that two years ago was part of the European crusade against the U.S. liberation of Iraq, offered a similar rethinking, with some historical comparison to an earlier U.S.-Europe schism:

> President Ronald Reagan's visit to Berlin in 1987 was, in many respects, very similar to President George W. Bush's visit to Mainz on Wednesday. . . . The Germany Reagan was traveling in, much like today's Germany, was very skeptical of the American President and his foreign policy. When Reagan stood before the Brandenburg Gate . . . and demanded that [Soviet leader Mikhail] Gorbachev "tear down this [Berlin] Wall," he was lampooned the next day on the editorial pages. He is a dreamer, wrote commentators. . . . Most experts agreed that his demand for the removal of the Wall was inopportune, utopian, and crazy. Yet three years later, East Germany had disappeared from the map. . . . Just a thought for Old Europe to chew on: Bush might be right, just like Reagan was then.

The Wisdom of Ordinary People

While we're distributing credit, the next bouquet needs to go to the everyday people of the Mideast. They have demonstrated, at times bravely, that even in long-suffering hellholes like Afghanistan, Iraq, and Palestine, there are many reasonable citizens willing to stand up for goodness. In missing this human reality, the timid, faithless, and sometimes craven "realists" who spent the last few years scorning the idea of democracy in the Middle East made a fundamental misjudgment. Their deepest error . . . is to place undeserved confidence in the opinions of elites, while doubting the political wisdom of the common man. My colleague [political scientist] Leon Aron, an authority on the former Soviet Union, recently wrote sagely on this topic:

The strength of the democratic impulse should never be underestimated. Again and again, liberty's appeal has proved powerful enough to overcome great obstacles. Elites, professing to know how the masses really feel, have time and again predicted disillusionment with democracy and its abandonment by the citizens of poor nations. Yet, in the past decade, nearly all fledgling democracies have resisted slipping back into authoritarianism. As always in matters of liberty, ordinary people have proved far wiser, and infinitely more patient, than intellectuals. Today's emerging democracies have shown remarkable resilience under harsh conditions. The voters in these poor and incomplete democracies seem to have grasped—as have few journalists or experts—the essence of [British philosopher] Isaiah Berlin's adage: "Liberty is liberty, not equality, or justice, or culture, or human happiness or a quiet conscience." Democracy itself, even amidst hardship, is cherished by consistent and solid majorities.

Today's snobs are just the latest in a long train of doubters of ordinary citizens. Almost 150 years ago, Abraham Lincoln battled such men while campaigning for the Senate. In a speech that has been wonderfully preserved in handwritten form, with Lincoln's spoken emphases underlined by him in ink (and replicated in the extract below) the first Republican President said this:

> Most governments have been based, practically, on the denial of the equal rights of men. . . . Ours began by affirming those rights.
>
> They said some men are too ignorant and vicious to share in government. Possibly so, said we; and by your system, you would always keep them ignorant and vicious.
>
> We proposed to give all a chance; and we expected the weak to grow stronger, the ignorant wiser, and all better, and happier together.

That's a pointed endorsement of the power of democratic self-responsibility to elevate both individuals and societies.

And it's as relevant to today's Middle East as it was to slave-holding America.

Let us never forget that peace and freedom start with superior firepower.

Peace Begins with Superior Firepower

Of course, good everyday citizens will only raise their hands if someone first suppresses the bullies in their midst. The reason reformers in the Middle East are finally coming out of the woodwork is because, as a *Washington Post* column recently acknowledged, "the new U.S. democratization policy, far from being an unwanted imposition, has given them a voice, an audience, and at least a partial shield against repression—three things they didn't have a year ago." Which brings us to our third set of heroes: U.S. fighting forces.

In the Middle East, as in most places where democracy has taken root, the ballot inspectors, television commentators, cajoling politicians, and buzzing new parliaments were all preceded by a vital prerequisite: some good men with rifles. In this case, good men from places like Mohrsville, Pennsylvania; Stockton, California; Round Rock, Texas; and Saranac Lake, New York. All the lilting speeches and learned counsel, the grand plans and inspiring coalitions are just will-o'-the-wisps until someone brave does the difficult duty of establishing the ground rules of liberty. Let us never forget that peace and freedom start with superior firepower.

There is little grandeur in that work. No one gets wealthy doing it. Some of the servicemen have only a hazy notion of the deeper stakes they are fighting for.

But those who reported for duty, including many who suffered and died, are now being paid in the transcendent coin of having created one of history's turning points.

4

U.S.-Imposed Democracy Cannot Succeed in the Middle East

Wesley Clark

Wesley Clark retired after thirty-four years in the U.S. military in 2000 at the rank of four-star general. From 1997 to 2000, he was NATO Supreme Allied Commander-in-Chief of the U.S. European Command. Clark was a Democratic candidate for U.S. president in 2004 but withdrew his candidacy. His most recently published works include Waging Modern War: Bosnia, Kosovo, and the Future of Combat *and* Winning Modern War: Iraq, Terrorism and the American Empire.

The George W. Bush administration's assertion that the demand for democracy in various countries of the Middle East is a direct result of the U.S. military intervention in Iraq is nonsense. Although the U.S. armed forces deserve credit for providing security during the Iraq elections, the U.S. invasion of Iraq has caused immense destruction and many civilian deaths that have increased anti-Americanism throughout the world. There is a strong resistance among the Middle Eastern peoples to U.S.-imposed democracy. Democratic reformers in the Middle East do not want their hopes and dreams dominated by America's political agenda. The United States should support the courageous local leaders in the Middle East and realize that democracy must be homegrown.

Wesley Clark, "War Didn't, and Doesn't Bring Democracy. (Middle East Democracy: Who Gets the Credit? What Are the Lessons?)," *Washington Monthly*, vol. 27, May 2005, pp. 22–25. Copyright 2005 by Washington Monthly Publishing, LLC, 733 15th St. NW, Suite 520, Washington, DC 20005. (202) 393–5155. Website: www.washington monthly.com. Reproduced by permission.

Operating on the theory that if you say something enough times people will believe it, the [George W.] Bush administration and its allies have in the last few years confidently put forth an array of assertions, predictions, and rationalizations about Iraq that have turned out to be nonsense. They've told us that [Iraqi dictator] Saddam's regime was on the verge of building nuclear weapons; that it had operational links with [terrorist group] al Qaeda; that our allies would support our invasion if we stuck with our insistence about going it alone; that we could safely invade with a relatively small number of ground troops; that the Iraqi people would greet us as liberators; that Ahmed Chalabi[1] could be trusted; that Iraq's oil revenues would pay for the country's reconstruction; and that most of our troops would be out of Iraq within six months of the initial invasion.

Now, they tell us that recent stirrings of democracy elsewhere in the Middle East are a direct consequence of our invasion of Iraq, that the neoconservative vision of contagious democracy has been realized. Given the administration's track record, we would be wise to greet this latest assertion with suspicion.

[The U.S. invasion of Iraq] has ... damaged America's reputation in the world ... and left our troops exposed in a hostile country with an open-ended exit strategy.

Negative Consequences of the U.S. Invasion

It's understandable that the administration would want to make this claim. After all, by any honest accounting, the Iraq operation has been a mess. The U.S. military has performed brilliantly for the most part. But we invaded the country for the express purpose of removing weapons of mass destruction

1. Ahmed Chalabi, former head of the Iraqi National Congress, gave false information to the U.S. government about Saddam Hussein's having weapons of mass destruction.

that turned out not to exist. That effort has cost $200 billion and more than 1,500 American lives. It has strained our alliances, damaged America's reputation in the world, pushed the all-volunteer military to the breaking point, and left our troops exposed in a hostile country with an open-ended exit strategy. It would be convenient to be able to say that the intent all along was just to bring democracy to the region and that this was simply the necessary price.

Convenient, but not true.

Certainly, the sight of Iraqis voting on January 30 [2005] was welcome, and a tremendous credit to the U.S. military efforts to provide security (though it was the Iraqis themselves who were most determined to hold the elections then, rather than delay the vote). The image of those purple Iraqi fingers was a powerful reminder that democracy knows no ethnic, religious, or geographic boundaries, and that freedom-loving hearts beat just as soundly under Arab robes as they do under grey suits.

At the same time, the demonstration effect of those elections has to be weighed against the immense damage our invasion has done in the region. Intensification of anti-Americanism and the ability of regional leaders to point to the chaos in Iraq as a reason to maintain the stability of current regimes are just some of the negative consequences of our invasion and occupation of Iraq.

Washington Falsely Takes Credit

Anyone who has traveled regularly to the Middle East over the years, as I have, knows that the recent hopeful democratic moves in Lebanon, Egypt, and the Palestinian territories have causal roots that long predate our arrival in Iraq, or that are otherwise unconnected to the war. American groups like the National Endowment for Democracy and numerous international organizations have been working with and strengthening reform-minded elements in these countries for years, and to some extent we are now seeing the fruits of that quiet involvement. But it is a mistake to believe that everything that is happening in the region—whether positive or negative—is a result of American military actions or rhetoric from Washington.

In Iran, for instance, the hopeful movement toward democracy went into remission after we invaded neighboring Iraq. Did our invasion cause democratic reform to falter in Iran? Not necessarily. There are many reasons—most of them internal—for why reform movements within a country wax and wane. But it is hard to claim that the Bush administration's invasion of Iraq was responsible for pro-democratic reactions in some Middle Eastern countries, but not for anti-democratic reactions in others.

Each of the positive developments that are currently bringing hope to the Middle East was more directly the result of a catalyzing local event than the consequence of American foreign policy. The death of [Palestinian Authority president] Yasser Arafat made possible the democratic breakthrough within the Palestinian Authority [PA] and the progress we're now seeing between the PA and Israel. In Lebanon, it took the assassination of former Prime Minister [Rafiq] Hariri and the outrage, both internal and international, that followed to spur Syrian withdrawal. And across the region, leaders like Egyptian President Hosni Mubarak have recognized the need to seek greater legitimacy by opening the door for democracy in order to stave off mounting threats from Islamic fundamentalists.

Although it may come as a surprise to . . . us here, there is a passionate resistance to the U.S. "imposing" its style of democracy.

The administration has generally responded to these openings by adding to the pressure, calling for withdrawal of Syrian forces and for democracy. But like the rooster who thinks his crowing caused the dawn, those who rule Washington today have a habit of taking credit for events of which they were in fact not the primary movers. Many of them have insisted, for instance, that the fall of the Berlin Wall in 1989 was largely the consequence of President Reagan's military policies. As a military officer at the time, and a Reagan supporter, I would be happy to give the Gipper that credit. In truth, however, our military posture was only one factor. As in the Middle East today, individuals who labored for freedom within these countries performed the bulk of the work. [Polish leader] Lech Walesa, [Czech leader] Vaclav Havel, and other contemporaries looked at America as an ideal, not as the muscle on every street corner. Other, truly transformative agents of Western influence, such as Pope John Paul II, the labor union movement, international commercial institutions, and the influences of next-door neighbors like the Federal Republic of Germany were at work.

Democracy can't be imposed—it has to be homegrown.

Democracy Cannot Be Imposed

Today, American democratic values are admired in the Middle East, but our policies have generated popular resentment. Although it may come as a surprise to those of us here, there is a passionate resistance to the U.S. "imposing" its style of democracy to suit American purposes. Democratic reformers in the Middle East don't want to have their own hopes and dreams subordinated to the political agenda of the United States. It's for this reason that the administration shouldn't try to take too much credit for the coming changes. Or be too boastful about our own institutions. Or too loud in proclaiming that we're thrilled about Middle Eastern democracy—mostly because it makes us feel safer. A little humility is likely to prove far more useful than chest-thumping.

As we work to help establish the conditions for democracy in Iraq, our most useful role elsewhere is surely behind the scenes. For example, the situation in Lebanon creates a power vacuum which could lead to the same kind of instability that ignited civil war there 30 years ago. We can, and should, be working diplomatically to provide the support, balance, and reassurances necessary for the revival of independent democracy in Lebanon. We should engage Syria to encourage cooperation in Iraq and liberalize its politics at home. At the very least, we should be helping to craft what comes next before we tighten the noose further on an already-shaky [Syrian president Hafiz al-] Assad. In our eagerness to help, we'd do well to heed the motto of my Navy friends in the submarine service: "Run silent-run deep."

Democracy can't be imposed—it has to be homegrown. In the Middle East, democracy has begun to capture the imagination of the people. For Washington to take credit is not only to disparage courageous leaders throughout the region, but also to undercut their influence at the time it most needs to be augmented. Let's give credit where credit is due—and leave the political spin at the water's edge.

5

Democracy in Iraq
Can Succeed

Adeed Dawisha

Born and raised in Iraq, Adeed Dawisha is a professor of political science at Miami University in Oxford, Ohio. He is also the author of Arab Nationalism in the Twentieth Century: From Triumph to Despair *(2003) as well as numerous articles.*

The January 2005 election represented a major political milestone in Iraqi history as a majority of Iraq's electorate voted in a democratic election for the first time in more than fifty years. Although the development of a new government has lagged and been marred by violence, Iraq's democratic future still looks hopeful. The major political actors who participated in the elections chose to negotiate with each other rather than use brute force. And although some commentators have been critical of the continued ethnosectarian divisions in Iraq, there is reason to be optimistic that the Iraqis will be able to develop a system of checks and balances that will overcome these divisions.

On 30 January 2005, eight and a half million Iraqis (almost 60 percent of Iraq's electorate) flocked to polling places in defiance of threats and assaults leveled against them by murderous groups of radical Islamists, remnants of [former Iraqi dictator] Saddam Hussein's defunct security services, and numbers of Sunni Arabs bent on using violence to reverse their recent loss of centuries-old status and privileges. Voters

Adeed Dawisha, "The New Iraq: Democratic Institutions and Performance," *Journal of Democracy*, vol. 16, July 2005. Copyright © 2005 The Johns Hopkins University Press. Reproduced by permission.

chose a National Assembly from a diverse array of political parties, groups, and coalitions ranging from Islamists to communists. Only Iraqis nearing the age of seventy could claim to have done anything like this before, as the last relatively free elections had taken place in June 1954—a distant memory that struck few chords among a disproportionately youthful populace whose only political recollection had been the years of debilitating tyranny under Saddam. The January 30 elections were indeed a seminal event in Iraqi History. . . .

Tempered Outlook

After more than three months of exhausting negotiations [since the January 2005 election], the exuberance and high or even inflated expectations that Iraqis displayed in the days immediately following their remarkable elections have given way to a more tempered outlook. Early hopes that a government would quickly take shape later curdled into disillusionment at the unlovely spectacle of parties scrambling and stalling to serve narrow interests while the brutal and resilient insurgency became ever bolder.

While it is understandable that citizens and observers should feel somewhat let down that the postelectoral talks took so long and featured so much zealous jostling for advantage, it would be wrong to conclude that any of this spells an irredeemably bleak future for Iraq. Some things, of course, have gone badly and give pause. The level of ethnosectarian tension on display is worrisome. Compromises came mostly at the margins, while core issues remained unresolved and are sure to come up again. The ratification of a new permanent constitution and the holding of general elections by June 2006 set an absolute deadline. Negotiations held and bargains struck over the next year will have to face all the hard issues. That various contending interests could dig in deep enough to cause disastrous deadlocks is a possibility that no responsible analyst can rule out. A lack of moderation over the next months could blight Iraq's political future for years to come, and the collateral damage inflicted on the cause of democratization could be severe.

[The Shi'ite and Kurd leaders may] even welcome a new ethos in which disagreements are settled less through brute strength than through discussion.

Hopeful Future

Yet there is a positive side to the story as well. As hard as they were to watch at times, the long weeks of horse trading after January's vote did feature the various parties working in a dedicated fashion to achieve their goals through peaceful political bargaining under the aegis of democracy. A large reason for the much-bemoaned delay, let us recall, was the UIA's [Shi'ite United Iraqi Alliance] evidently sincere desire to include as many groups as possible. The UIA's leaders could, after all, fairly easily have leveraged their slim majority into a quickly formed but narrowly based government. Similarly, while Kurdish stubbornness over Kirkuk[1] cost a month's delay, the very willingness of the Kurds to talk—when they could simply have sent a hundred thousand armed men into the city and presented the fledgling National Assembly with a *fait accompli*—may itself be a healthy sign. The willingness of the Shi'ite and Kurdish leaders to approach problems politically may have simply been the result of a rational realization that they could not force matters. But it could also be that they accept or even welcome a new ethos in which disagreements are addressed less through brute strength than through discussion and conciliation.

Many commentators and politicians from the Arab world outside Iraq have condemned the degree to which Iraqis seem

1. Kirkuk is a city in northern Iraq from which about 100,000 Kurds were expelled during Saddam Hussein's regime. When the Iraq war began in 2003, some Kurdish forces briefly occupied the city.

concerned with ethnic and sectarian issues. These outsiders claim that subnational bonds were irrelevant in the era before March 2003, when Iraqi nationalism supposedly reigned and the only relevant identity in the land between and around the Tigris and the Euphrates was "Iraqi." This of course is sheer fantasy. The truth is that Iraq was a country divided along ethnic and sectarian lines—indeed, Saddam was an expert at playing on such divisions through both force and fraud in order to perpetuate his dictatorial rule and with it the privileges of his own in-group. The fall of Saddam did not bring these cleavages to Iraq, and their reality must be confronted.

Iraq's very [ethnosectarian] divisions, if properly handled could become . . . an impetus for the growth of resilient democratic and pluralist institutions.

The question is not *whether* Iraq is divided, but rather *how* these divisions will affect the country's future. One possibility is that the intercommunal divisions will widen and harden, creating conditions of irreconcilable conflict that could lead to secession or even war. The insurgents have been carrying out their killings with the apparent hope of bringing such an outcome closer with every murder and explosion. Another and more hopeful prospect is that Iraq's very divisions, if properly handled, could become the mainspring of and incentive for a system of checks and balances, and through them an impetus for the growth of resilient democratic and pluralist institutions. This would be a happy irony, to be sure, but history has seen stranger ones.

6

Democracy in Iraq Will Fail

Robert Fisk

Robert Fisk is the Middle East correspondent for the British newspaper The Independent. *His published works include* The Great War for Civilization: The Conquest of the Middle East *(2005) and* Pity the Nation: The Abduction of Lebanon *(2002).*

The reality on the streets of Iraq belies the assertions made by President George W. Bush and British prime minister Tony Blair that democracy is succeeding in the Middle East. Iraq is in a state of complete anarchy, torn apart by violent ethnic conflict. Although the Western media continues to remind the Iraqi people about how grateful they should be to be rid of former dictator Saddam Hussein, the Iraqis have much more immediate concerns. Living in hardship, terror, and tragedy, they are not fooled by Western leaders' empty rhetoric about democratic progress in the Middle East.

It makes you want to scream. I have been driving the dingy, dangerous, oven-like streets of Baghdad all week, ever more infested with insurgents and their informers, the American troops driving terrified over the traffic islands, turning their guns on all of us if we approach within 50 meters.

In the weird, space-ship isolation of [former Iraqi dictator] Saddam's old republican palace, the Kurds [Iraqi ethnic minority] and the Shia [minority Muslim denomination] have been tearing Iraq apart, refusing to sign up for a constitution lest it fail to give them the federations—and the oil wealth—they want. They miss their deadline—though I found no one in "real" Baghdad, no one outside the Green Zone bunker, who seemed to care.

And that evening, I turn on my television to hear President [George W.] Bush praise the "courage" of the constitution negotiators whose deadline Bush himself had promised would be met.

Courage? So it's courageous, is it, to sit in a time capsule, sealed off from your people by miles of concrete walls, and argue about the future of a nation which is in anarchy. Then [U.S. secretary of state] Condoleezza Rice steps forward to tell us this is all part of the "road to democracy" in the Middle East.

Myth vs. Reality

I am back on the streets again, this time at the an-Nahda bus station—*nahda* means renaissance for those who want the full irony of such situations—and around me is the wreckage of another bombing. Smashed police cars, burnt-out, pulverised buses (passengers all on board, of course), women screaming with fury, children taken to the al-Kindi hospital in bandages to be met by another bomb.

Your city may suffer 1,100 violent deaths in [one month] alone, . . . but just to take your mind off things, remember that Saddam [Hussein] is going on trial.

And that night, I flip on the television again and find the local US military commander in the Sadr City district of Baghdad—close to the bus station—remarking blithely that while local people had been very angry, they supported the local "security" forces (ie, the Americans) and were giving them more help than ever and that we were—wait for it—"on the path to democracy".

Sometimes I wonder if there will be a moment when reality and myth, truth and lies, will actually collide. When will the detonation come? When the insurgents wipe out an entire US base? When they pour over the walls of the Green Zone and turn it into the same trashed blocks as the rest of Baghdad? Or will we then be told—as we have been in the past—that this just shows the "desperation" of the insurgents, that these terrible acts (the bus station bombing . . . , for example) only prove that the "terrorists" know they are losing?

The people of Baghdad . . . have more fears, more anxieties and greater mourning to endure than any offer of bread and circuses by the Americans can assuage.

Saddam Hussein Is a Thing of the Past

In a traffic jam, a boy walks past my car, trying to sell a magazine. Saddam's face—yet again—is on the cover. The ex-dictator's seedy, bewhiskered features are on the front pages, again and again, to remind the people of Baghdad how fortunate they are to be rid of the dictator. Saddam to go on trial next month, in two months' time, before the end of the year [2005].

Six deadlines for the ghastly old man's trial have come and gone—like so many other deadlines in Iraq—but the people are still supposed to be fascinated and appalled at Saddam's picture. You may sweat at home in powerless houses; you may have no fresh food because your freezer is hot; you may have to queue for hours to buy petrol; you may have to suffer constant death threats and armed robbery and your city may suffer 1,100 violent deaths in July [2005] alone (all true) but, just to take your mind off things, remember that Saddam is going on trial.

I have not met anyone in Iraq—save for those who lost their loved ones to his thugs—who cares any more about Saddam. He is yesterday's man, a thing of the past. To conjure up this monster again is an insult to the people of Baghdad—who have more fears, more anxieties and greater mourning to endure than any offer of bread and circuses by the Americans can assuage.

Charade of Democracy

Yet in the outside world—the further from Iraq, the more credible they sound—George Bush and Lord Blair of Kut al-Amara[1], will repeat that we really have got democracy on its feet in Iraq, that we overthrew the tyrant Saddam and that a great future awaits the country and that new investments are being planned at international conferences (held far away from Iraq, of course) and that the next bombings in Europe, like the last ones, will have nothing—absolutely nothing—to do with Iraq.

The show must go on and I know, when I return to Beirut [Lebanon] or fly to Europe, Iraq will not look so bad. The Mad Hatter will look quite sane and the Cheshire Cat will smile at me from the tree.

It is to their eternal credit that those who live in the hell of Iraq . . . are not fooled by the nonsense peddled by George Bush.

Democracy, democracy, democracy. Take Egypt. President [Hosni] Mubarak allows opponents in the forthcoming elections. Bush holds this up as another sign of democracy in the Middle East. But Mubarak's opponents have to be approved by his own party members in parliament, and the Muslim Brotherhood—which ought to be the largest party in the country—is still officially illegal. Sitting in Baghdad, I watched

1. Fisk refers to British Prime Minister Tony Blair and the humiliating defeat of the British by the Ottomans in World War I, which occurred in Kut al-Amara, south of Baghdad.

Mubarak's first party rally, a mawkish affair in which he actually asked for support. So who will win this "democratic" election? I'll take a risk: our old pal Mubarak. And I'll bet he gets more than 80 per cent of the votes. Watch this space. [He got 88%.]

And of course, from my little Baghdad eyrie I've been watching the eviction of Israelis from their illegal settlements in the Palestinian Gaza Strip. The word "illegal" doesn't pop up on the BBC [British Broadcasting Corp.], of course; nor the notion that the settlers—for which read colonisers—were not being evicted from their land but from land they originally took from others. Nor is much attention paid to the continued building in the equally illegal colonies within the Palestinian West Bank which will—inevitably—make a "viable" (Lord Blair's favourite word) Palestine impossible.

In Gaza, everyone waited for Israeli settler and Israeli soldier to open fire on each other. But when a settler did open fire, he did so to murder four Palestinian workers on the West Bank. The story passed through the television coverage like a brief, dark, embarrassing cloud and was forgotten. Settlements dismantled. Evacuation from Gaza. Peace in our time.

But in Baghdad, the Iraqis I talk to are not convinced. It is to their eternal credit that those who live in the hell of Iraq still care about the Palestinians, still understand what is really happening in the Middle East, are not fooled by the nonsense peddled by George Bush and Lord Blair of Kut al-Amara. "What is this 'evil ideology', that Blair keeps talking about?" an Iraqi friend asked me. "What will be your next invention? When will you wake up?"

I couldn't put it better myself.

7

Islamic Culture Provides a Sound Basis for Democracy

Bernard Lewis

British historian Bernard Lewis is a professor of Near Eastern Studies at Princeton University. He has published more than twenty books on Islam and the Middle East, including What Went Wrong: Western Impact and Middle East Response *(2002),* The Crisis of Islam: Holy War and Unholy Terror *(2003), and* From Babel to Dragonians: Interpreting the Middle East *(2004).*

Critics who say that the Middle East and Muslim societies have always been ruled by tyrannical authoritarian regimes have misread history. In fact, the principles of equality and consultation and the duty to depose unjust authority have been part of the Islamic tradition since the religion was founded in the seventh century. Regimes like those of former Iraqi dictator Saddam Hussein are alien to Islamic traditions and have resulted from the influence of Western modernization, German nazism, and Soviet communism. Leaders of Middle Eastern countries can draw from Islamic traditions to construct democratic governments.

For Muslims as for others, history is important, but they approach it with a special concern and awareness. The career of the Prophet Muhammad, the creation and expansion of the Islamic community and state, and the formulation and elaboration of the holy law of Islam are events in history, known from historical memory or record and narrated and debated by historians since early times. In the Islamic Middle East, one may still find passionate arguments, even bitter feuds, about events that occurred centuries or sometimes millennia ago—about what happened, its significance, and its current relevance. This historical awareness has acquired new dimensions in the modern period, as Muslims—particularly those in the Middle East—have suffered new experiences that have transformed their vision of themselves and the world and reshaped the language in which they discuss it.

Equality among believers was a basic principle of Islam from its foundation in the seventh century.

Islam and Equality

In 1798, the French Revolution arrived in Egypt in the form of a small expeditionary force commanded by a young general called Napoleon Bonaparte. The force invaded, conquered, and ruled Egypt without difficulty for several years. General Bonaparte proudly announced that he had come "in the name of the French Republic, founded on the principles of liberty and equality." This was, of course, published in French and also in Arabic translation. Bonaparte brought his Arabic translators with him, a precaution that some later visitors to the region seem to have overlooked.

The reference to equality was no problem: Egyptians, like other Muslims, understood it very well. Equality among believers was a basic principle of Islam from its foundation in the seventh century, in marked contrast to both the caste system of India to the east and the privileged aristocracies of the Christian world to the West. Islam really did insist on equality and achieved a high measure of success in enforcing it. Obviously, the facts of life created inequalities—primarily social and economic, sometimes also ethnic and racial—but these were in defiance of Islamic principles and never reached the levels of the Western world. Three exceptions to the Islamic rule of equality were enshrined in the holy law: the inferiority of slaves, women, and unbelievers. But these exceptions were not so remarkable; for a long time in the United States, in practice if not in principle, only white male Protestants were "born free and equal." The record would seem to indicate that as late as the nineteenth or even the early twentieth century, a poor man of humble origins had a better chance of rising to the top in the Muslim Middle East than anywhere in Christendom, including post-revolutionary France and the United States.

Just as ... Westerners thought of good government and bad government as freedom and slavery, so Muslims conceived of them as justice and injustice.

Islam and Freedom

Equality, then, was a well-understood principle, but what about the other word Bonaparte mentioned—"liberty," or freedom? This term caused some puzzlement among the Egyptians. In Arabic usage at that time and for some time after, the word "freedom"—*hurriyya*—was in no sense a political term. It was a legal term. One was free if one was not a slave. To be liberated, or freed, meant to be manumitted [set free from slavery], and in the Islamic world, unlike in the Western world, "slavery" and "freedom" were not until recently used as metaphors for bad and good government.

The puzzlement continued until a very remarkable Egyptian scholar found the answer. Sheikh Rifa'a Rafi' al-Tahtawi was a professor at the still unmodernized al-Azhar University of the early nineteenth century. The ruler of Egypt had decided it was time to try and catch up with the West, and in 1826 he sent a first mission of 44 Egyptian students to Paris. Sheikh Tahtawi accompanied them and stayed in Paris until

1831. He was what might be called a chaplain, there to look after the students' spiritual welfare and to see that they did not go astray—no mean task in Paris at that time.

During his stay, he seems to have learned more than any of his wards, and he wrote a truly fascinating book giving his impressions of post-revolutionary France. The book was published in Cairo in Arabic in 1834 and in a Turkish translation in 1839. It remained for decades the only description of a modern European country available to the Middle Eastern Muslim reader. Sheikh Tahtawi devotes a chapter to French government, and in it he mentions how the French kept talking about freedom. He obviously at first shared the general perplexity about what the status of not being a slave had to do with politics. And then he understood and explained. When the French talk about freedom, he says, what they mean is what we Muslims call justice. And that was exactly right. Just as the French, and more generally Westerners, thought of good government and bad government as freedom and slavery, so Muslims conceived of them as justice and injustice. These contrasting perceptions help shed light on the political debate that began in the Muslim world with the 1798 French expedition and that has been going on ever since, in a remarkable variety of forms.

Islamic Nation of Justice

As Sheikh Tahtawi rightly said, the traditional Islamic ideal of good government is expressed in the term "justice." This is represented by several different words in Arabic and other Islamic languages. The most usual, *adl*, means "justice according to the law" (with "law" defined as God's law, the sharia as revealed to the Prophet [Muhammad] and to the Muslim community). But what is the converse of justice? What is a regime that does not meet the standards of justice? If a ruler is to qualify as just, as defined in the traditional Islamic system of rules and ideas, he must meet two requirements: he must have acquired power rightfully, and he must exercise it rightfully. In other words, he must be neither a usurper nor a tyrant. It is of course possible to be either one without the other, although the normal experience was to be both at the same time.

The Islamic notion of justice is well documented and goes back to the time of the Prophet. The life of the Prophet Muhammad, as related in his biography and reflected in revelation and tradition, falls into two main phases. In the first phase he is still living in his native town of Mecca [in modern-day Saudi Arabia] and opposing its regime. He is preaching a new religion, a new doctrine that challenges the pagan oligarchy that rules Mecca. The verses in the Koran, and also relevant passages in the prophetic traditions and biography, dating from the Meccan period, carry a message of opposition—of rebellion, one might even say of revolution, against the existing order.

Muslims have been interested from the very beginning in the problems of politics and government.

Then comes the famous migration, the *hijra* from Mecca to Medina [in Saudi Arabia], where Muhammad becomes a wielder, not a victim, of authority. Muhammad, during his lifetime, becomes a head of state and does what heads of state do. He promulgates and enforces laws, he raises taxes, he makes war, he makes peace; in a word, he governs. The political tradition, the political maxims, and the political guidance of this period do not focus on how to resist or oppose the government, as in the Meccan period, but on how to conduct government. So from the very beginning of Muslim scripture, jurisprudence, and political culture, there have been two distinct traditions: one, dating from the Meccan period, might be called activist; the other, dating from the Medina period, quietist.

Obedience and Opposition to Authority

The Koran, for example, makes it clear that there is a duty of obedience: "Obey God, obey the Prophet, obey those who hold authority over you." And this is elaborated in a number of sayings attributed to Muhammad. But there are also sayings that put strict limits on the duty of obedience. Two dicta attributed to the Prophet and universally accepted as authentic are indicative. One says, "there is no obedience in sin"; in other words, if the ruler orders something contrary to the divine law, not only is there no duty of obedience, but there is a duty of disobedience. This is more than the right of revolution that appears in Western political thought. It is a duty of revolution, or at least of disobedience and opposition to authority. The other pronouncement, "do not obey a creature against his creator," again clearly limits the authority of the ruler, whatever form of ruler that may be.

These two traditions, the one quietist and the other activist, continue right through the recorded history of Islamic states and Islamic political thought and practice. Muslims have been interested from the very beginning in the problems of politics and government: the acquisition and exercise of power, succession, legitimacy, and—especially relevant here— the limits of authority.

All this is well recorded in a rich and varied literature on politics. There is the theological literature; the legal literature, which could be called the constitutional law of Islam; the practical literature—handbooks written by civil servants for civil servants on how to conduct the day-to-day business of government; and, of course, there is the philosophical literature, which draws heavily on the ancient Greeks, whose work was elaborated in translations and adaptations, creating distinctly Islamic versions of Plato's *Republic* and Aristotle's *Politics*.

In the course of time, the quietist, or authoritarian, trend grew stronger, and it became more difficult to maintain those limitations on the autocracy of the ruler that had been prescribed by holy scripture and holy law. And so the literature places increasing stress on the need for order. A word used very frequently in the discussions is *fitna*, an Arabic term that can be translated as "sedition," "disorder," "disturbance," and even "anarchy" in certain contexts. The point is made again and again, with obvious anguish and urgency: tyranny is better than anarchy. Some writers even go so far as to say that an hour—or even a moment—of anarchy is worse than a hundred years of tyranny. That is one point of view—but not the only one. In some times and places within the Muslim world, it has been dominant; in other times and places, it has been emphatically rejected.

The Tradition of Consultation

The Islamic tradition insists very strongly on two points concerning the conduct of government by the ruler. One is the need for consultation. This is explicitly recommended in the Koran. It is also mentioned very frequently in the traditions of the Prophet. The converse is despotism; in Arabic *istibdad*, "despotism" is a technical term with very negative connotations. It is regarded as something evil and sinful, and to accuse a ruler of istibad is practically a call to depose him.

The traditional system of Islamic government is both consensual and contractual.

With whom should the ruler consult? In practice, with certain established interests in society. In the earliest times, consulting with the tribal chiefs was important, and it remains so in some places—for example, in Saudi Arabia and in parts of Iraq (but less so in urbanized countries such as Egypt or Syria). Rulers also consulted with the countryside's rural gentry, a very powerful group, and with various groups in the city: the bazaar merchants, the scribes (the nonreligious literate classes, mainly civil servants), the religious hierarchy, and the military establishment, including long-established regimental groups such as the janissaries of the Ottoman Empire.[1] The importance of these groups was, first of all, that they did have real power. They could and sometimes did make trouble for the ruler, even deposing him. Also, the groups' leaders—tribal chiefs, country notables, religious leaders, heads of guilds, or commanders of the armed forces—were not nominated by the ruler, but came from within the groups.

Consultation is a central part of the traditional Islamic order, but it is not the only element that can check the ruler's authority. The traditional system of Islamic government is both consensual and contractual. The manuals of holy law generally assert that the new caliph—the head of the Islamic community and state—is to be "chosen." The Arabic term used is sometimes translated as "elected," but it does not connote a general or even sectional election. Rather, it refers to a small group of suitable, competent people choosing the ruler's successor. In principle, hereditary succession is rejected by the juristic tradition. Yet in practice, succession was always hereditary, except when broken by insurrection or civil war; it was—and in most places still is—common for a ruler, royal or otherwise, to designate his successor.

Consent of the Ruled

But the element of consent is still important. In theory, at times even in practice, the ruler's power—both gaining it and maintaining it—depends on the consent of the ruled. The basis of the ruler's authority is described in the classical texts by the Arabic word *bay'a*, a term usually translated as "homage," as in the subjects paying homage to their new ruler. But a more accurate translation of *bay'a*—which comes from a verb meaning "to buy and to sell"—would be "deal," in other words,

---

1. In the Ottoman Empire (1389–1826), male children from non-Muslim communities were recruited as slave soldiers into special corps called "janissaries."

a contract between the ruler and the ruled in which both have obligations.

Some critics may point out that regardless of theory, in reality a pattern of arbitrary, tyrannical, despotic government marks the entire Middle East and other parts of the Islamic world. Some go further, saying, "That is how Muslims are, that is how Muslims have always been, and there is nothing the West can do about it." That is a misreading of history. One has to look back a little way to see how Middle Eastern government arrived at its current state.

Modernizing meant introducing Western systems of . . . rule, inevitably including the tools of domination and repression.

Impact of Modernization

The change took place in two phases. Phase one began with Bonaparte's incursion and continued through the nineteenth and twentieth centuries when Middle Eastern rulers, painfully aware of the need to catch up with the modern world, tried to modernize their societies, beginning with their governments. These transformations were mostly carried out not by imperialist rulers, who tended to be cautiously conservative, but by local rulers—the sultans of Turkey, the pashas and khedives of Egypt, the shahs of Persia—with the best of intentions but with disastrous results.

Modernizing meant introducing Western systems of communication, warfare, and rule, inevitably including the tools of domination and repression. The authority of the state vastly increased with the adoption of instruments of control, surveillance, and enforcement far beyond the capabilities of earlier leaders, so that by the end of the twentieth century any tinpot ruler of a petty state or even of a quasi state had vastly greater powers than were ever enjoyed by the mighty caliphs and sultans of the past.

But perhaps an even worse result of modernization was the abrogation of the intermediate powers in society—the landed gentry, the city merchants, the tribal chiefs, and others—which in the traditional order had effectively limited the authority of the state. These intermediate powers were gradually weakened and mostly eliminated, so that on the one hand the state was getting stronger and more pervasive, and on the other hand the limitations and controls were being whittled away.

This process is described and characterized by one of the best nineteenth-century writers on the Middle East, the British naval officer Adolphus Slade, who was attached as an adviser to the Turkish fleet and spent much of his professional life there. He vividly portrays this process of change. He discusses what he calls the old nobility, primarily the landed gentry and the city bourgeoisie, and the new nobility, those who are part of the state and derive their authority from the ruler, not from their own people. "The old nobility lived on their estates," he concludes. "The state is the estate of the new nobility." This is a profound truth and, in the light of subsequent and current developments, a remarkably prescient formulation.

Imported Ideology

The second stage of political upheaval in the Middle East can be dated with precision. In 1940, the government of France surrendered to Nazi Germany. A new collaborationist government was formed and established in a watering place called Vichy [in central France], and General Charles de Gaulle moved to London and set up a Free French committee. The French empire was beyond the reach of the Germans at that point, and the governors of the French colonies and dependencies were free to decide: they could stay with Vichy or rally to de Gaulle. Vichy was the choice of most of them, and in particular the rulers of the French-mandated territory of

Syria-Lebanon, in the heart of the Arab East. This meant that Syria-Lebanon was wide open to the Nazis, who moved in and made it the main base of their propaganda and activity in the Arab world.

It was at that time that the ideological foundations of what later became the Baath Party were laid, with the adaptation of Nazi ideas and methods to the Middle Eastern situation. The nascent party's ideology emphasized pan-Arabism, nationalism, and a form of socialism. The party was not officially founded until April 1947, but memoirs of the time and other sources show that the Nazi interlude is where it began. From Syria, the Germans and the proto-Baathists also set up a pro-Nazi regime in Iraq, led by the famous, and notorious, Rashid Ali al-Gailani.

To speak of dictatorship as being the immemorial way of doing things [in Muslim countries] . . . shows ignorance of the Arab past.

The Rashid Ali regime in Iraq was overthrown by the British after a brief military campaign in May–June 1941. Rashid Ali went to Berlin, where he spent the rest of the war as Hitler's guest with his friend the mufti of Jerusalem, Haj Amin al-Husseini. British and Free French forces then moved into Syria, transferring it to Gaullist control. In the years that followed the end of World War II, the British and the French departed, and after a brief interval the Soviets moved in.

The leaders of the Baath Party easily switched from the Nazi model to the communist model, needing only minor adjustments. This was a party not in the Western sense of an organization built to win elections and votes. It was a party in the Nazi and Communist sense, part of the government apparatus particularly concerned with indoctrination, surveillance, and repression. The Baath Party in Syria and the separate Baath Party in Iraq continued to function along these lines.

Since 1940 and again after the arrival of the Soviets, the Middle East has basically imported European models of rule: fascist, Nazi, and communist. But to speak of dictatorship as being the immemorial way of doing things in that part of the world is simply untrue. It shows ignorance of the Arab past, contempt for the Arab present, and unconcern for the Arab future. The type of regime that was maintained by [former Iraqi dictator] Saddam Hussein—and that continues to be maintained by some other rulers in the Muslim world—is modern, indeed recent, and very alien to the foundations of Islamic civilization. There are older rules and traditions on which the peoples of the Middle East can build.

8

Islamic Culture Is Not Compatible with Democracy

Roger Scruton

Roger Scruton is a British writer and philosopher. Formerly a professor of philosophy at Boston University, his published works include fiction, philosophy, and political and cultural commentary. His most recent books include The West and the Rest *(2002) and* Gentle Regrets: Thoughts from a Life *(2005).*

For Muslims of the Middle East (except Turkey), the Koran is the final authority on all matters and offers the path to salvation. According to the Koran, Muslims should not be loyal to any country, constitution, or secular law, but should only be loyal to God and the teachings of the holy scripture. Because Islam is based on decrees of the Koran, there is no room for the negotiations and compromises that characterize a democracy. Historically, democracy has not developed in the Middle East because Islamic culture is in conflict with the tenets of democracy, including free speech and secular law.

[For Muslims] the Koran is considered the final authority on all matters it touches upon—and that means just about all matters that impinge on the lives of ordinary mortals. Its style is exhortatory, and its mood imperative. It resounds with threats and imprecations and, for all its many passages of lyrical beauty, it is the biggest joke-free zone in literature. It occupies the space reserved in the human psyche

Roger Scruton, "Religion of Peace?: Islam Without the Comforting Clichés," *National Review*, vol. 54, December 31, 2002. Copyright © 2002 by National Review, Inc., 215 Lexington Avenue, New York, NY 10016. Reproduced by permission.

for obedience, and leaves no room for any merely human jurisdiction. The Koranic conception of law as holy law, pointing the unique way to salvation and applying to every area of human life, therefore involves a confiscation of the political. Those matters which, in Western societies, are resolved by negotiation, compromise, and the laborious work of offices and committees are the object of immovable and eternal decrees. The rules are either laid down explicitly in the holy book or discerned there by some religious figurehead—whose authority, however, can always be questioned by some rival imam, or jurist, since the shari'a (holy law) recognizes no office or institution as endowed with any independent lawmaking power. The shari'a, moreover, is addressed to the faithful, wherever and with whomsoever they find themselves; it does not merely bind Muslims but isolates them from the secular society by which they are surrounded. In any crisis secular law will count for nothing, since the law of God eclipses it.

Contrast with Christianity

The contrast with Christianity is instructive. St. Paul, who turned the ascetic and self-denying religion of Christ into an organized form of worship, was a Roman citizen, versed in the law, who shaped the early Church through the legal idea of the *universitas*, or corporation. The Pauline Church was designed not as a sovereign body, but as a universal citizen, entitled to the protection of the secular and imperial powers but with no claim to displace those powers as the source of legal order. This corresponds to Christ's own vision in the parable of the tribute money: "Render therefore to Caesar the things that are Caesar's; and unto God the things that are God's." The Church has therefore tended to recognize the business of governing human society as a human business, and the Christian as both a servant of God and a citizen of the secular order. It is a distinctive Christian achievement to propose secular government as a religious duty, and religious toleration as an avenue to God. The Enlightenment conception of the citizen, as joined in a free social contract with his neighbors under a tolerant and secular rule of law, derives directly from the Christian legacy.

This contrasts radically with the vision set before us in the Koran, according to which sovereignty rests with God and his Prophet, and legal order is founded in divine command. True law is holy law, whose precepts derive from the four sources of Islamic legal thought: the Koran, the Sunna (customs authorized by the Prophet), qiyas ("analogy"), and ijma' ("consensus"). These are the sources to which the classical jurists referred when giving judgment, and they none of them acknowledge any law-making institution of merely human provenance. They are the means for discerning God's will, and so attaining the posture of submission (the literal meaning of *islam*).

The democratic idea has not taken root [in the Islamic world] . . . because [Muslim] culture, habits and institutions make no room for it.

No Room for Democracy

When Islam first spread across the Middle East and the Southern Mediterranean, it was not by preaching and conversion in the Christian manner, but by conquest. The conquered peoples were given the choice: believe or die. Exceptions were made for the "people of the Book" (Christians, Jews, and Zoroastrians), who could enjoy the subordinate status of *dhimmi*—i.e., being protected by treaty. But the treaty offered no right to worship, and forbade all attempts to proselytize. Other religions existed within the dar al-islam [land of Islam] on sufferance, and religious toleration was regarded as a regrettable expedient rather than a political virtue.

Under the Ottoman Empire[1] Islam steadily lost both its belligerent attitude to other faiths and its ability to maintain itself through religious law. In the 19th century the Ottoman sultans began to borrow laws, institutions, and secular customs from the West, so that when the empire collapsed after World War I, its center was able to jettison the perimeter and reshape itself as a modern secular state on the Western model. Thus was born modern Turkey, the creation of [Turkey's founder and first president] Kernal Ataturk, and the one durable democracy in the Muslim world. Turkey endures as a democracy because it has secularized its institutions and excluded the clergy from power. In no sense, however, can it be seen as the product of a Muslim "Enlightenment," equivalent to the Enlightenment that transformed the legal and political order of Europe. Turkey is a deliberately Westernized state.

Elsewhere in the Islamic world the democratic idea has not taken root—not because people have rejected it, but because their culture, habits, and institutions make no room for it. Secular government is kept in place by dictatorship, or by ruthless expedients that confer no legitimacy but only power on those who deploy them. In the Middle East, dictatorships designed to retain power in the hands of a single person, a single family, or a single dominant tribe exist side by side with a near-universal nostalgia for another and purer form of government, in which the holy law delivered to the Prophet will bring lasting peace and justice under the rule of God.

[The Islamist ideal] recognizes no loyalty to dynasty, territory or secular law, but only to God and His promises.

It has often been said that Islam has turned its back on modernity, which it cannot encompass through its law and doctrine. And to some extent this is true, the efforts of West-

---

1. The large and powerful Muslim empire covering the Middle East and North Africa from 1299–1922.

ernizers and legal reformers notwithstanding. Much more important, however, is the intense longing for that original and pure community once promised by the Prophet but betrayed repeatedly by his worldly successors and followers. Like every form of nostalgia, this longing involves a turning away from reality, a refusal to accommodate or even to perceive the facts that might undermine it, and an endlessly renewable anger against the Other who refuses to share in the collective dream. This is the mood that inspires the Muslim Brotherhood in Egypt, the Wahhabi sect in Saudi Arabia, and the Shi'ite revival of [fundamentalist clerical leader] Ayatollah Khomeini [in Iran]. And it is the mood that animates the Islamist terrorists.

Muslims Repress Dissent

Rulers of Islamic states are aware of the danger posed by this immovable nostalgia. They know that it recognizes no loyalty to dynasty, territory, or secular law, but only to God and His promises. Hence they ruthlessly suppress the Islamist movements in their midst—as [Syrian president] Hafez al-Assad suppressed the Muslim Brotherhood in the town of Hama in Syria, leaving 10,000 dead and a great medieval town in ruins. Similar measures have been taken in Egypt, Iraq, Tunisia, Algeria, and Saudi Arabia. But the threat is always there, and the measures must always be renewed. . . .

Western societies [on the other hand] tolerate and even welcome dissent, and our disputes are resolved through compromise and dialogue. Thanks to our Christian legacy we see political action not as a means to achieve the kingdom of God on earth, but as a way of maintaining equilibrium between people who share a territory but who may not share a religion, and whose conflicts can be resolved through a common national loyalty and a common territorial law. None of that is accepted by the Islamists.

9

Many in the Middle East Are Eager for Democracy

Fouad Ajami

Fouad Ajami is a Lebanese-born American professor of Middle Eastern Studies at the School for Advanced International Studies at Johns Hopkins University. His published works include The Arab Predicament *and* The Dream Palace of the Arabs: A Generation's Odyssey.

After decades of being mired in a culture of tyranny and oppression, the people of the Middle East are becoming receptive to the idea of freedom. The revolutionary message brought to them by U.S. president George W. Bush—that the Arab and Muslim world can achieve freedom and democracy—has created a new impetus for democratic change. In Iraq, for example, the citizens are working hard to create a democratic government and develop a free press. Though the insurgents continue to try to derail this progress, no one believes they will succeed. Everywhere in the Middle East the old order is under attack and the people are embracing the principles of democracy.

"George W. Bush has unleashed a tsunami on this region," a shrewd Kuwaiti merchant who knows the way of his world said to me. The man had no patience with the standard refrain that Arab reform had to come from within, that a foreign power cannot alter the age-old ways of the Arabs. "Everything here—the borders of these states, the oil explorations that remade the life of this world, the political outcomes that favored the elites now in the saddle—came from the outside. This moment of possibility for the Arabs is no exception." A Jordanian of deep political experience at the highest reaches of Arab political life had no doubt as to why history suddenly broke in Lebanon, and could conceivably change in Syria itself before long. "The people in the streets of Beirut knew that no second Hama is possible; they knew that the rulers were under the gaze of American power, and knew that Bush would not permit a massive crackdown by the men in Damascus."

My informant's reference to Hama was telling: It had been there in 1982, in that city of the Syrian interior, that the Baathist-Alawite regime had broken and overwhelmed Syrian society. Hama had been a stronghold of the Muslim Brotherhood, a fortress of the Sunni middle class. It had rebelled, and the regime unleashed on it a merciless terror. There were estimates that 25,000 of its people perished in that fight. Thenceforth, the memory of Hama hung over the life of Syria—and Lebanon. But the people in the plazas of Beirut, and the Syrian intellectuals who have stepped forth to challenge the Baathist regime, have behind them the warrant, and the green light, of American power and protection.

Unmistakably, there is in the air of the Arab world a new contest about the possibility and the meaning of freedom.

To venture into the Arab world, as I did recently over four weeks in Qatar, Kuwait, Jordan and Iraq, is to travel into Bush Country. I was to encounter people from practically all Arab lands, to listen in on a great debate about the possibility of freedom and liberty. I met Lebanese giddy with the Cedar Revolution that liberated their country from the Syrian prison that had seemed an unalterable curse. They were under no illusions about the change that had come their way. They knew

73

that this new history was the gift of an American president who had put the Syrian rulers on notice. The speed with which Syria quit Lebanon was astonishing, a race to the border to forestall an American strike that the regime could not discount. I met Syrians in the know who admitted that the fear of American power, and the example of American forces flushing [former Iraqi dictator] Saddam Hussein out of his spider hole, now drive Syrian policy. They hang on George Bush's words in Damascus, I was told: the rulers wondering if Iraq was a crystal ball in which they could glimpse their future.

The weight of American power, historically on the side of the dominant order, now drives this new quest among the Arabs. For decades, the intellectual classes in the Arab world bemoaned the indifference of American power to the cause of their liberty. Now a conservative American president had come bearing the gift of Wilsonian redemption. For a quarter century the Pax Americana had sustained the autocracy of Egyptian President Hosni Mubarak: He had posed as America's man on the Nile, a bulwark against the Islamists. He was sly and cunning, running afoul of our purposes in Iraq and over Israeli-Palestinian matters. He had nurtured a culture of anti-modernism and anti-Americanism, and had gotten away with it. Now the wind from Washington brought tidings: America had wearied of Mr. Mubarak, and was willing to bet on an open political process, with all its attendant risks and possibilities. The brave oppositional movement in Cairo that stepped forth under the banner of *Kifaya* ("Enough!") wanted the end of his reign: It had had enough of his mediocrity, enough of the despotism of an aging officer who had risen out of the military bureaucracy to entertain dynastic dreams of succession for his son. Egyptians challenging the quiescence of an old land may have had no kind words to say about America in the past. But they were sure that the play between them and the regime was unfolding under Mr. Bush's eyes.

Unmistakably, there is in the air of the Arab world a new contest about the possibility and the meaning of freedom. This world had been given over to a dark nationalism, and to the atavisms of a terrible history. For decades, it was divided between rulers who monopolized political power and intellectual classes shut out of genuine power, forever prey to the temptations of radicalism. Americans may not have cared for those rulers, but we judged them as better than the alternative. We feared the "Shia bogeyman" in Iraq and the Islamists in Algeria, Egypt and Tunisia; we bought the legend that Syria's dominion in Lebanon kept the lid on anarchy. We feared tinkering with the Saudi realm; it was terra incognita to us, and the House of Saud seemed a surer bet than the "wrath and virtue" of the zealots. Even [Palestinian leader] Yasser Arafat, a retailer of terror, made it into our good graces as a man who would tame the furies of the masked men of [Palestinian terrorist group] Hamas. That bargain with authoritarianism did not work, and begot us the terrors of 9/11.

The revolutionary message [President Bush] brought forth was . . . there [is] no Arab and Muslim "exceptionalism" to the appeal of liberty.

Appeal of Liberty

The children of Islam, and of the Arabs in particular, had taken to the road, and to terror. There were many liberal, secular Arabs now clamoring for American intervention. The claims of sovereignty were no longer adequate; a malignant political culture had to be "rehabilitated and placed in receivership," a wise Jordanian observer conceded. Mr. Bush may not be given to excessive philosophical sophistication, but his break with "the soft bigotry of low expectations" in the Arab-Islamic world has found eager converts among Muslims and Arabs keen to repair their world, to wean it from a culture of scapegoating and self-pity. Pick up the Arabic papers today:

They are curiously, and suddenly, readable. They describe the objective world; they give voice to recognition that the world has bypassed the Arabs. The doors have been thrown wide open, and the truth of that world laid bare. Grant Mr. Bush his due: The revolutionary message he brought forth was the simple belief that there was no Arab and Muslim "exceptionalism" to the appeal of liberty. For a people mired in historical pessimism, the message of this outsider was a powerful antidote to the culture of tyranny. Hitherto, no one had bothered to tell the Palestinians that they can't have terror and statehood at the same time, that the patronage of the world is contingent on a renunciation of old ways. This was the condition Mr. Bush attached to his support for the Palestinians. It is too early to tell whether the new restraint in the Palestinian world will hold. But it was proper that Mr. Bush put Arafat beyond the pale.

There was [in the Iraqi National Assembly] the spectacle of democracy: men and women doing democracy's work.

Democracy in Action

It was Iraq of course that gave impetus to this new Arab history. And it is in Iraq that the nobility of this American quest comes into focus. This was my fourth trip to Iraq since the fall of the despotism, and my most hopeful yet. I traveled to Baghdad, Kirkuk, Erbil and Suleimaniyah. A close colleague—Leslie Gelb, president emeritus of the Council on Foreign Relations—and I were there to lecture and to "show the flag." We met with parliamentarians and journalists, provincial legislators, clerics and secularists alike, Sunni and Shia Arabs and Kurds. One memory I shall treasure: a visit to the National Assembly. From afar, there are reports of the "acrimony" of Iraq, of the long interlude between Iraq's elections, on Jan. 30 [2005], and the formation of a cabinet. But that day, in the assembly, these concerns seemed like a quibble with history.

There was the spectacle of democracy: men and women doing democracy's work, women cloaked in Islamic attire right alongside more emancipated women, the technocrats and the tribal sheikhs, and the infectious awareness among these people of the precious tradition bequeathed them after a terrible history. One of the principal leaders of the Supreme Islamic Council for Revolution in Iraq, Sheikh Hamam Hammoudi, an elegant, thoughtful cleric in his early 50s, brushed aside the talk of a Shia theocracy. This Shia man, who knew a smattering of English, offered his own assurance that the example and the power of Iran shall be kept at bay: "My English is better than my Farsi, even though I spent 20 years in Iran." He was proud of his Iraqi identity, proud of being "an Arab." He was sure that the Najaf school of Shia jurisprudence would offer its own alternative to the world view of [the Iranian city of] Qom, across the border. He wanted no theocratic state in Iraq: Islam, he said, would be "a source" of legislation, but the content of politics would be largely secular. The model, he added, with a touch of irony, would be closer to the American mix of religion and politics than to the uncompromising secularism of France.

There is to this moment in Arab history the feel of a reenactment of Europe's Revolution of 1848—the springtime of peoples.

Insurgents Are History

The insurgents were busy with their bombs and their plots of mayhem: Georgian troops [troops from Georgia trained by U.S. military to serve in Iraq] guarded the National Assembly and controlled access to it. But a people were taking to a new political way. A woman garbed in black, a daughter of a distinguished clerical Shia family, made the rounds among her fellow legislators. Religious scruples decreed that she could not shake the hand of a male stranger. But she was proud and wily, a free woman in a newly emancipated polity. She let me know how much she knew about the ways and the literature of the West. American power may have turned on its erstwhile ally, Ahmed Chalab[1]. But his appearance in the assembly's gallery drew to him parliamentarians of every stripe. He, too, had about him the excitement of this new politics.

A lively press has sprouted in Iraq: There is an astonishing number of newspapers and weeklies, more than 250 in all. There are dozens of private TV channels and radio stations. Journalists and editors speak of a press free of censorship. Admittedly, the work is hard and dangerous, the logistics a veritable nightmare. But no single truth claimed this country, no "big man" sucked the air out of its public life. The insurgents will do what they are good at. But no one really believes that those dispensers of death can turn back the clock. Among the Sunni Arabs, there is growing recognition that the past cannot be retrieved, that it had been a big error to choose truculence and political maximalism. By a twist of fate, the one Arab country that had seemed ever marked for brutality and sorrow now stands poised on the frontier of a new political world. No Iraqis I met look to neighboring Arab lands for political inspiration: They are scorched by the terror and the insurgency, but a better political culture is tantalizingly close.

The Gift of Liberty

Women are getting the vote in Kuwait, the Lebanese clamor for the truth about the assassination of former prime minister Rafiq Hariri, and about the dark Syrian interlude in their history. Egyptians don't seem frightened of the scarecrows with which the Mubarak regime secured their submission. Everywhere, the order is under attack, and men and women are willing to question the prevailing truths. There is to this moment of Arab history the feel of a reenactment of Europe's

1. Head of Iraq's National Congress, Chalabi was considered a valuable U.S. ally until the information he provided about Saddam Hussein's weapons of mass destruction proved to be false.

Revolution of 1848—the springtime of peoples: That revolution broke out in France, then spread to the Italian states, to the German principalities, to the remotest corners of the Austrian empire. There must have been 50 of these revolts—rebellions of despair and of contempt. History was swift: The revolutions spread with velocity and were turned back with equal speed. The fear of chaos dampened these rebellions.

As I made my way on this Arab journey, I picked up a meditation that Massimo d'Azeglio, a Piedmontese [Italian] aristocrat who embraced that "springtime" in Europe, offered about his time, which speaks so directly to this Arab time: "The gift of liberty is like that of a horse, handsome, strong, and high-spirited. In some it arouses a wish to ride; in many others, on the contrary, it increases the desire to walk." It would be fair to say that there are many Arabs today keen to walk—frightened as they are by the prospect of the Islamists coming to power and curtailing personal liberties, snuffing out freedoms gained at such great effort and pain. But more Arabs, I hazard to guess, now have the wish to ride.

10

Many in the Middle East Favor Authoritarian, Islamist Regimes

Fareed Zakaria

An Indian-born Muslim and former professor of political science at Harvard University, Fareed Zakaria is editor of Newsweek International. *He writes regularly for the* New York Times, Newsweek, *and the* Wall Street Journal. *His most recent book,* The Future of Freedom *(2003), was a* New York Times *best-seller.*

President George W. Bush's strategy to bring democracy to the Middle East in order to create societies that uphold the basic freedoms and rights of their citizens needs to be reassessed. Although many commentators thought Islamic fundamentalists were losing their foothold in the region, events in 2005 proved otherwise. Many people in the Arab world continue to support authoritarian regimes and to elect anti-Western fundamentalists. Although some fundamentalists have begun to work through democratic channels, they continue to reject Western values like liberalism, tolerance, and freedom. The tension that has developed between the people's desire for democracy and lack of respect for liberty is at the heart of the current fiasco in the Middle East.

George W. Bush is not a man for second thoughts, but even he might have had some recently. Ever since 9/11, Bush has made the promotion of democracy in the Middle

East the center-piece of his foreign policy, and doggedly pushed the issue. However, this approach has borne strange fruit, culminating in [the Islamic extremist group] Hamas's victory in [the 2005 elections in] Gaza and the West Bank [Palestinian Territories].

Before that, we have watched it strengthen [extremist group] Hizbullah in Lebanon, which (like Hamas) is often described in the West as a terrorist organization. In Iraq, the policy has brought into office conservative religious parties with their own private militias. In Egypt, it has bolstered the Muslim Brotherhood, one of the oldest fundamentalist organizations in the Arab world, from which Al Qaeda [Islamist terrorist group] descends. "Democracies replace resentment with hope, respect the rights of their citizens and their neighbors, and join the fight against terror," Bush said [in January 2006] in his State of the Union address. But is this true of the people coming to power in the Arab world today?

It is the violence of the response in some parts of the Muslim world that suggests a rejection of the ideas of tolerance and freedom.

Democracy vs. Liberty

This is an issue that deserves serious thought, well beyond pointing to the awkwardness of Bush's position. Bush's prescription is, after all, one accepted by many governments: it is also European policy to push for democratic reform in the Middle East. And in fact, little has happened that makes the case for continued support of Muslim dictatorships. But events do powerfully suggest that if we don't better understand the history, culture and politics of the countries that we are "reforming," we will be in for an extremely rocky ride.

There is a tension in the Islamic world between the desire for democracy and a respect for liberty. (It is a tension that

81

once raged in the West and still exists in pockets today.) This is most apparent in the fury [in early 2006] over the publication of cartoons of the Prophet Muhammad in a small Danish newspaper. The cartoons were offensive and needlessly provocative. Had the paper published racist caricatures of other peoples or religions, it would also have been roundly condemned and perhaps boycotted. But the cartoonist and editors would not have feared for their lives. It is the violence of the response in some parts of the Muslim world that suggests a rejection of the ideas of tolerance and freedom of expression that are at the heart of modern Western societies.

Why are all these strains rising now? Islamic fundamentalism was supposed to be on the wane. [In 2001] the best scholars of the phenomenon were writing books with titles like "The Failure of Political Islam." Observers pointed to the exhaustion of the Iranian revolution, the ebbing of support for radical groups from Algeria to Egypt to Saudi Arabia. And yet one sees political Islam on the march across the Middle East today. Were we all wrong? Has Islamic fundamentalism gotten a second wind?

Fundamentalists Turning to Democracy

There are those who argue that the collapse of the Arab-Israeli peace process, the war on terror, and the bloodshed in Afghanistan and Iraq have all contributed to the idea that Islam is under siege—providing radicals with fresh ammunition. This is not, however, a wholly convincing case. For one thing, opposition to the Iraq war is not a radical phenomenon in the Middle East, but rather an utterly mainstream one. Almost every government opposed it. Moreover, the rise and fall of Islamic fundamentalism was a broad and deep phenomenon, born over decades. It could hardly reverse itself on the basis of a year's news. Does anyone believe that if there had been no Iraq war, Hamas would have lost? Or that the Danish cartoons would have been published with no response?

The political Islamist movement has changed over the last 15 years. Through much of the 1980s and 1990s, Islamic fundamentalists had revolutionary aims. They sought the violent overthrow of Western-allied regimes to have them replaced with Islamic states. This desire for Islamic states and not Western-style democracies was at the core of their message. Often transnational in their objectives, they spoke in global terms. But it turned out that the appeal of this ideology was limited. People in Algeria, Egypt, Saudi Arabia and countless other places rejected it; in fact, they grudgingly accepted the dictatorships they lived under rather than support violent extremism. In this sense, political Islam did fail.

But over time, many of the Islamists recognized this reality and began changing their program. They came to realize that shorn of violent overthrow, revolution and social chaos, their ideas could actually gain considerable popular support. So they reinvented themselves, emphasizing not revolutionary overthrow but peaceful change, not transnational ideology but national reform. They were still protesting the dictators, but now they organized demonstrations in favor of democracy and honest politics.

This coming to terms with democracy . . . should not be mistaken for a coming to terms with Western values such as liberalism, tolerance and freedom.

Liberalism, Tolerance, and Freedom Thwarted

There were extremist elements, of course, still holding true to the cause of the caliphate [the fundamentalist view that all Muslims should be ruled by one leader], and they broke off to create separate groups like [terrorist group] Al Qaeda. (Some of this radicalism remains within the diaspora communities of Europe more strongly than in the Middle East itself.) But it is notable that well before 9/11, Egypt's Muslim Brotherhood condemned terrorism directed against the Mubarak regime, and it recently distanced itself even from the tactics of the Iraqi insurgency. It has sought instead to build support for its own social and political program in Egypt. For its part, not only did Hamas decide to participate in the elections—for the first time—but it campaigned almost entirely on a platform of anticorruption, social services and assertive nationalism. Only Al Qaeda and its ilk have condemned any participation in elections, whether by Iraqi Islamist groups or by Hamas.

This coming to terms with democracy, however, should not be mistaken for a coming to terms with Western values such as liberalism, tolerance and freedom. The program that most of these groups espouse is deeply illiberal, involving the reversal of women's rights, second-class citizenship for minorities and confrontation with the West and Israel. The most dramatic example of these trends is in southern Iraq, where Shiite [a Muslim minority] religious parties rule without any checks. Reports abound that civil servants and professors are subjected to religious and political tests, women are placed under strictures never before enforced in Iraq, and all kinds of harmless entertainment are being silenced by vigilantes. When entering the office of Iraq's prime minister, Ibrahim Jaafari, one now sees women swaddled in veils and gloves, a level of zeal rarely seen elsewhere in the Muslim world.

In face of the powerlessness, alienation and confusion that the modern world breeds, [Islamist] groups simply say, "Islam is the solution."

Islam As the Solution

Some of these forces have gained strength because of a lack of other alternatives. For decades the Middle East has been a political desert. In Iraq, the reason that there are no countervailing liberal parties is that [former Iraqi dictator] Saddam Hussein destroyed them. He could not completely crush mosque-based groups and, by the end of his reign, he actually used them to shore up his own legitimacy. In much of the Muslim world Islam became the language of political opposition because it was the only language that could not be censored. This pattern, of dictators using religious groups to destroy the secular opposition, played itself out in virtually every Arab country, and often beyond. It was the method by which Pakistan's [former president] Gen. Zia ul-Haq maintained his own dictatorship in the 1980s, creating a far stronger fundamentalist movement than that country had ever known.

The broader reason for the rise of Islamic politics has been the failure of secular politics. Secularism exists in the Middle East. It is embodied by Saddam Hussein and [Libyan dictator] Muammar Kaddafi and [Egyptian president] Hosni Mubarak and [now-deceased Palestinian leader] Yasir Arafat. Arabs believe that they have tried Western-style politics and it has brought them tyranny and stagnation. They feel that they got a bastardized version of the West and that perhaps the West was not the right model for them anyway. Islamic fundamentalism plays deeply to these feelings. It evokes authenticity, pride, cultural assertiveness and defiance. These ideas have been powerful sources of national identity throughout history and remain so, especially in an age of globalized economics and American power. In face of the powerlessness, alienation and confusion that the modern world breeds, these groups say simply, "Islam is the solution."

Five candidates took part in the most recent [Iranian election]. The pro-Western liberal came in fifth; the conservative West-basher came in first.

Inevitably we have to ask ourselves what to do about these movements that are rising to power. The first task is surely to understand them—understand that they thrive on pride and a search for authenticity. These forces play themselves out in complex ways. It is obvious by now that the United States—and Europe as well—understand countries like Iraq and Iran very little. In Iraq, the United States overturned old social structures and governing patterns with little thought as to what would replace them. We believed that democracy and freedom would solve the problems of disorder, division and dysfunction.

Iran As a Complex Case

Or consider Iran. Many Americans had become convinced that the vast majority of Iranians hated their regime and were trying desperately to overthrow it; all we needed to do was help them foment a revolution. There's little doubt that the regime is brutal and unpopular. But it also appears to have some basis of support, in mosques, patronage systems and poorer parts of the country. And those who do not support it are not automatically Western liberals. After all, there was an election in Iran and, despite low turnout, the eventual vote was free and secret. (Back when the winner of Iranian elections was a liberal, Mohammed Khatami, people often cited the vote as proof that the fundamentalists were failing.) Five candidates took part in the most recent race. The pro-Western liberal came in fifth; the conservative West-basher came in first.

My own guess, and it is just a guess, is that some Iranians—not a majority, but not a tiny minority, either—accept their current regime. This is partly because of its ideology and patronage politics, and partly because of general inertia. (We have only to look at Iraq to see that Shiite religious figures do have some hold on their populations.) Add to this an apparatus of repression and $60-a-barrel oil and you have a regime that has many ways to stay in power. President [Mahmoud] Ahmadinejad understands these forces. He emphasizes in his daily television appearances not Islamic dogma but poverty alleviation, subsidies, anti-corruption projects and, above all, nationalism in the form of the nuclear program. Ahmadinejad may be a mystic, but most of his actions are those of a populist, using the forces that will work to keep him in power. This picture of Iran, gray and complex, is much less satisfying than the black-and-white caricature. But it might be closer to the truth.

Promoting Liberty Is Essential

Elections have not created political Islam in the Middle East. They have codified a reality that existed anyway. Hamas was already a major player to be reckoned with in Gaza. The Muslim Brotherhood is popular in Egypt, whether or not Hosni Mubarak holds real elections. In fact, the more they are suppressed, the greater their appeal. If politics is more open, these groups may or may not moderate themselves, but they will surely lose some of that mystical allure they now have. The martyrs will become mayors, which is quite a fall in status.

But to accept these forces is not to celebrate them. It is important that religious intolerance and antimodern attitudes not be treated as cultural variations that must be respected. Whether it is Hindu intolerance in India, anti-Semitism in Europe or Muslim bigotry in Saudi Arabia, the modern world rightly condemns them all as violating universal values. Recent months have only highlighted that promoting democracy and promoting liberty in the Middle East are separate projects. Both have their place. But the latter—promoting the forces of political, economic and social liberty—is the more difficult and more important task. And unless we succeed at it, we will achieve a series of nasty democratic outcomes, as we are beginning to in so many of these places.

This fight is not one the fundamentalists are destined to win. The forces of liberalism have been stymied in the Middle East for decades. They need help. Recall that in Europe for much of the last 100 years, when liberal democrats were not given assistance, nationalists and communists often triumphed through the democratic processes.

Above all, the forces of moderation thrive in an atmosphere of success. Two Muslim societies in which there is little extremism are Turkey and Malaysia. Both are open politically and thriving economically. Compare Pakistan today—growing at 8 percent a year—with General Zia's country, and you can see why; for all the noise, fundamentalism there is waning. If you are comfortable with the modern world, you are less likely to want to blow it up.

Forging a Real Partnership

There are better and worse ways to handle radical Islam. We should not feed the fury that helps them win adherents. The Bush administration's arrogance has been a great boon to the nastiest groups in the Middle East, which are seen as the only ones who can stand up to the imperial bully. We should recognize how varied these groups are: some violent, others not, some truly anti-modern, others not—and work to divide rather than unite them. When, for example, Bush added Chechen brutalities to his list of crimes of "radical Islam," he made a mistake. Russia has waged a horrific war against Chechnya for two decades, killing more than 100,000 civilians. To speak of that conflict in the same breath as the [July 2005] London bombings [by Islamic terrorists], as Bush did, is to suggest that any time a Muslim kills, whatever the provocation, it's all the same to him.

Give Bush his due. He has correctly and powerfully argued that blind assistance to the dictatorships of the Middle East was a policy that was producing repression and instability. But he has not yet found a way to genuinely assist in the promotion of political, economic and social reforms in the region. A large part of the problem is that the United States—and the West in general—are not seen as genuine well-wishers and allies of the peoples of these countries in their aspirations for a better life. We have stopped partnering with repressive Middle Eastern regimes, but we have not yet managed to forge a real partnership with Middle Eastern societies.

11

Women's Rights Are Essential to Democracy in the Middle East

Pippa Norris and Ronald Inglehart

Pippa Norris is a political scientist at Harvard University's John F. Kennedy School of Government and Ronald Inglehart is a political scientist at the Institute for Social Research at the University of Michigan. Norris and Inglehart coauthored Rising Tide: Gender Equality and Cultural Change Around the World *(2003) and* Sacred And Secular: Religion and Politics Worldwide *(2004).*

Although people in the Muslim world pay lip service to the ideal of democracy, they do not share the core values required for the successful implementation and sustainment of democracy. These values include social tolerance, trust between people, and the belief in the equal rights of men and women. A society's attitudes towards gender equality is a reliable indicator of the extent to which democracy can succeed. Successful democratic reform in the Middle East must therefore include promoting women's rights.

Democracy promotion in Islamic countries is now one of the [George W.] Bush administration's most popular talking points. "We reject the condescending notion that freedom will not grow in the Middle East," [former] Secretary of State Colin Powell declared [in December 2002] as he unveiled the White House's new Middle East Partnership Initiative to encourage political and economic reform in Arab countries. Likewise, Condoleezza Rice, formerly President George W. Bush's national security advisor [and currently secretary of state], promised [in September 2002] that the United States is committed to "the march of freedom in the Muslim world."

Democratic Values

But does the Muslim world march to the beat of a different drummer? Despite Bush's optimistic pronouncement that there is "no clash of civilizations" when it comes to "the common rights and needs of men and women," others are not so sure. [American political scientist] Samuel Huntington's controversial 1993 thesis—that the cultural division between "Western Christianity" and "Orthodox Christianity and Islam" is the new fault line for conflict—resonates more loudly than ever since [the terrorist attacks of] September 11 [2001]. Echoing Huntington, columnist Polly Toynbee argued in the British *Guardian* in November [2002], "What binds together a globalized force of some extremists from many continents is a united hatred of Western values that seems to them to spring from Judeo-Christianity." Meanwhile, on the other side of the Atlantic, Democratic Rep. Christopher Shays of Connecticut, after sitting through hours of testimony on U.S.-Islamic relations on Capitol Hill . . . , testily blurted, "Why doesn't democracy grab hold in the Middle East? What is there about the culture and the people and so on where democracy just doesn't seem to be something they strive for and work for?"

Huntington's response would be that the Muslim world lacks the core political values that gave birth to representative democracy in Western civilization: separation of religious and secular authority, rule of law and social pluralism, parliamentary institutions of representative government, and protection of individual rights and civil liberties as the buffer between citizens and the power of the state. This claim seems all too plausible given the failure of electoral democracy to take root throughout the Middle East and North Africa. According to the latest Freedom House rankings, almost two thirds of the 192 countries around the world are now electoral democracies. But among the 47 countries with a Muslim majority, only one fourth are electoral democracies—and none of the core Arabic-speaking societies falls into this category.

The real fault line between the West and Islam . . . concerns gender equality and sexual liberation.

Culture Does Matter

Yet this circumstantial evidence does little to prove Huntington correct, since it reveals nothing about the underlying beliefs of Muslim publics. Indeed, there has been scant empirical evidence of whether Western and Muslim societies exhibit deeply divergent values—that is, until now. The cumulative results of the two most recent waves of the World Values Survey (WVS), conducted in 1995–96 and 2000–2002, provide an extensive body of relevant evidence. Based on questionnaires that explore values and beliefs in more than 70 countries, the WVS is an investigation of sociocultural and political change that encompasses over 80 percent of the world's population.

A comparison of the data yielded by these surveys in Muslim and non-Muslim societies around the globe confirms the first claim in Huntington's thesis: Culture does matter—indeed, it matters a lot. Historical religious traditions have left an enduring imprint on contemporary values. However, Huntington is mistaken in assuming that the core clash between the West and Islam is over political values. At this point in history, societies throughout the world (Muslim and Judeo-Christian alike) see democracy as the best form of government. Instead, the real fault line between the West and Islam, which Huntington's theory completely overlooks, concerns gender equality and sexual liberation. In other words, the values separating the two cultures have much more to do with eros [sexuality] than demos [politics]. As younger generations in the West have gradually become more liberal on these issues, Muslim nations have remained the most traditional societies in the world.

The people of the Muslim world overwhelmingly want democracy, but democracy may not be sustainable in their societies.

A "Sexual Clash of Civilizations"

This gap in values mirrors the widening economic divide between the West and the Muslim world. Commenting on the disenfranchisement of women throughout the Middle East, the United Nations Development Programme observed that "no society can achieve the desired state of well-being and human development, or compete in a globalizing world, if half its people remain marginalized and disempowered." But this "sexual clash of civilizations" taps into far deeper issues than how Muslim countries treat women. A society's commitment to gender equality and sexual liberalization proves time and again to be the most reliable indicator of how strongly that society supports principles of tolerance and egalitarianism. Thus, the people of the Muslim world overwhelmingly want democracy, but democracy may not be sustainable in their societies.

Huntington argues that "ideas of individualism, liberalism, constitutionalism, human rights, equality, liberty, the rule of law, democracy, free markets, [and] the separation of church and state" often have little resonance outside the West. Moreover, he holds that Western efforts to promote these ideas provoke a violent backlash against "human rights imperialism." To test these propositions, we categorized the countries included in the WVS according to the nine major contemporary civilizations, based largely on the historical religious legacy of each society. The survey includes 22 countries representing Western Christianity (a West European culture that also encompasses North America, Australia, and New Zealand), 10 Central European nations (sharing a Western Christian heritage, but which also lived under Communist rule), 11 societies with a Muslim majority (Albania, Algeria, Azerbaijan, Bangladesh, Egypt, Indonesia, Iran, Jordan, Morocco, Pakistan, and Turkey), 12 traditionally Orthodox societies (such as Russia and Greece), 11 predominately Catholic Latin American countries, 4 East Asian societies shaped by Sino-Confucian values, 5 sub-Saharan African countries, plus Japan and India.

It's a step in the right direction if most people in a country endorse democracy. But this sentiment needs to be complemented by deeper underlying attitudes.

Democracy's Positive Image

Despite Huntington's claim of a clash of civilization between the West and the rest, the WVS reveals that, at this point in history, democracy has an overwhelmingly positive image throughout the world. In country after country, a clear majority of the population describes "having a democratic political system" as either "good" or "very good." These results represent a dramatic change from the 1930s and 1940s, when fascist regimes won overwhelming mass approval in many societies; and for many decades, Communist regimes had widespread support. But in the last decade, democracy became virtually the only political model with global appeal, no matter what the culture. With the exception of Pakistan, most of the Muslim countries surveyed think highly of democracy: In Albania, Egypt, Bangladesh, Azerbaijan, Indonesia, Morocco, and Turkey, 92 to 99 percent of the public endorsed democratic institutions—a higher proportion than in the United States (89 percent).

Yet, as heartening as these results may be, paying lip service to democracy does not necessarily prove that people genuinely support basic democratic norms—or that their leaders will allow them to have democratic institutions. Although constitutions of authoritarian states such as China profess to embrace democratic ideals such as freedom of religion, the rulers deny it in practice. In Iran's 2000 elections, reformist candidates captured nearly three quarters of the seats in parliament, but a theocratic elite still holds the reins of power. Certainly, it's a step in the right direction if most people in a country endorse democracy. But this sentiment needs to be complemented by deeper underlying attitudes such as interpersonal trust and tolerance of unpopular groups—and these values must ultimately be accepted by those who control the army and secret police.

Muslims Support Democratic Institutions

The WVS reveals that, even after taking into account differences in economic and political development, support for democratic institutions is just as strong among those living in Muslim societies as in Western (or other) societies. For instance, a solid majority of people living in Western and Muslim countries gives democracy high marks as the most efficient form of government, with 68 percent disagreeing with assertions that "democracies are indecisive" and "democracies aren't good at maintaining order." (All other cultural regions and countries, except East Asia and Japan, are far more critical.) And an equal number of respondents on both sides of the civilizational divide (61 percent) firmly reject authoritarian governance, expressing disapproval of "strong leaders" who do not "bother with parliament and elections." Muslim societies display greater support for religious authorities playing an active societal role than do Western societies. Yet this preference for religious authorities is less a cultural division between the West and Islam than it is a gap between the West and many other less secular societies around the globe, especially in sub-Saharan Africa and Latin America. For instance, citizens in some Muslim societies agree overwhelmingly with the statement that "politicians who do not believe in God are unfit for public office" (88 percent in Egypt, 83 percent in Iran, and 71 percent in Bangladesh), but this statement also garners strong support in the Philippines (71 percent), Uganda (60 percent), and Venezuela (52 percent). Even in the United States, about two fifths of the public believes that atheists are unfit for public office.

Support for gender equality—a key indicator of tolerance and personal freedom—is closely linked with a society's level of democracy

---

Gender Equality and Democracy

However, when it comes to attitudes toward gender equality and sexual liberalization, the cultural gap between Islam and the West widens into a chasm. On the matter of equal rights and opportunities for women—measured by such questions as whether men make better political leaders than women or whether university education is more important for boys than for girls—Western and Muslim countries score 82 percent and 55 percent, respectively. Muslim societies are also distinctively less permissive toward homosexuality, abortion, and divorce.

These issues are part of a broader syndrome of tolerance, trust, political activism, and emphasis on individaul autonomy that constitutes "self-expression values." The extent to which a society emphasizes self-expression values has a surprisingly strong bearing on the emergence and survival of democratic institutions. Among all the countries included in the WVS, support for gender equality—a key indicator of tolerance and personal freedom—is closely linked with a society's level of democracy.

Low Tolerance for Gender Equality

In every stable democracy, a majority of the public disagrees with the statement that "men make better political leaders than women." None of the societies in which less than 30 percent of the public rejects this statement (such as Jordan, Nigeria, and Belarus) is a true democracy. In China, one of the world's least democratic countries, a majority of the public agrees that men make better political leaders than women, despite a party line that has long emphasized gender equality. [Chinese revolutionary leader] Mao Zedong once declared, "women hold up half the sky"). In practice, Chinese women occupy few positions of real power and face widespread discrimination in the workplace. India is a borderline case. The country is a long-standing parliamentary democracy with an independent judiciary and civilian control of the armed forces, yet it is also marred by a weak rule of law, arbitrary arrests, and extrajudicial killings. The status of Indian women reflects this duality. Women's rights are guaranteed in the constitution, and [former prime minister] Indira Gandhi led the nation for 15 years. Yet domestic violence and forced prostitution remain prevalent throughout the country, and, according to the WVS, almost 50 percent of the Indian populace believes only men should run the government.

Divergent [cultural] values constitute the real clash between Muslim societies and the West.

Muslim societies are neither uniquely nor monolithically low on tolerance toward sexual orientation and gender equality. Many of the Soviet successor states rank as low as most Muslim societies. However, on the whole, Muslim countries not only lag behind the West but behind all other societies as well. Perhaps more significant, the figures reveal the gap between the West and Islam is even wider among younger age groups. This pattern suggests that the younger generations in

Western societies have become progressively more egalitarian than their elders, but the younger generations in Muslim societies have remained almost as traditional as their parents and grandparents, producing an expanding cultural gap.

Culture has a lasting impact on how societies evolve. But culture does not have to be destiny.

Values Crucial to Democracy

"The peoples of the Islamic nations want and deserve the same freedoms and opportunities as people in every nation," President Bush declared in a commencement speech at West Point [in 2002]. He's right. Any claim of a "clash of civilizations" based on fundamentally different political goals held by Western and Muslim societies represents an oversimplification of the evidence. Support for the goal of democracy is surprisingly widespread among Muslim publics, even among those living in authoritarian societies. Yet Huntington is correct when he argues that cultural differences have taken on a new importance, forming the fault lines for future conflict. Although nearly the entire world pays lip service to democracy, there is still no global consensus on the self-expression values—such as social tolerance, gender equality, freedom of speech, and interpersonal trust—that are crucial to democracy. Today, these divergent values constitute the real clash between Muslim societies and the West.

The United States cannot expect to foster democracy in the Muslim world simply by getting countries to adopt the trappings of democratic governance, such as holding elections and having a parliament. Nor is it realistic to expect that nascent democracies in the Middle East will inspire a wave of reforms reminiscent of the velvet revolutions that swept Eastern Europe in the final days of the Cold War. A real commitment to democratic reform will be measured by the willingness to commit the resources necessary to foster human development in the Muslim world. Culture has a lasting impact on how societies evolve. But culture does not have to be destiny.

12

Women's Rights Are Not Essential to Democracy in the Middle East

Marina S. Ottaway

Marina S. Ottaway is a senior associate for the Democracy and Rule of Law project at the Carnegie Endowment for International Peace in Washington, D.C. The purpose of the Democracy and Rule of Law project is to analyze the state of democracy around the world and the efforts by the United States and other countries to promote democracy. Ottaway's recently published books include Democracy Challenged: The Rise of Semi-authoritarianism *(2003), and* Uncharted Journey: Democracy Promotion in the Middle East, *coedited with Thomas Carothers (2005), from which the following viewpoint is excerpted.*

The U.S. government has promoted women's rights in the Middle East as an integral part of its strategy to bring democracy to the region. Although many Arab and American leaders applaud these efforts, there is no strong evidence that promoting women's rights is necessary for democratization in the Arab world. As an historical example, the United States and Great Britain began to develop democratic institutions long before women had the right to vote or participate in politics. In contrast, while some socialist countries have promoted rights of women, these countries also limited the democratic rights of all their citizens. Although it is important for women to have more rights in the Arab world, U.S. pressure on Arab countries to advance these rights will not advance democracy. Furthermore, promoting women's rights in the name of democracy may even be dangerous: It may alienate Middle Eastern conservatives who fear the moral impact of women's liberation on Islamic societies.

The U.S. government has made the promotion of women's rights and the empowerment of women a central element of its new campaign to modernize and democratize the Arab world. The Middle East Partnership Initiative (MEPI), the major aid program through which the United States seeks to facilitate the transformation of the Arab world, makes women's rights one of its priorities. No official U.S. speech about reform in the Middle East fails to mention the cause of women's rights. And the issue of women is sure to be raised at meetings where Middle East affairs are discussed, regardless of the main purpose of the gathering.

The new U.S. focus on women's rights and the position of women in the Arab world in general received strong encouragement by the publication of the United Nations Development Programme's *Arab Human Development Report 2002.* Signed by a number of prominent Arab intellectuals, the report drew a dismal picture of a region lagging behind the rest of the world because of major deficits in freedom, women's empowerment, and education. The report argued that the deficit in women's empowerment was not simply a problem of justice and equity, but a major cause of the Arab world's backwardness. "The utilization of Arab women's capabilities through political and economic participation remains the lowest in the world in quantitative terms, as evidenced by the very low share of women in parliaments, cabinets, and the work force, and in the trend toward the feminization of unemployment," the report explained. "Society as a whole suffers when a huge proportion of its productive potential is stifled. . . ." The argument has since been repeated by President George W. Bush and [his] administration officials. "No society can succeed and prosper while denying basic rights to the women of their country," declared President Bush in a May 2003 commencement speech at the University of South Carolina. Secretary of State Colin Powell echoed the sentiment arguing: "Until the countries of the Middle East unleash the abilities and potential of their women, they will not build a future of hope."

[We caution] against the assumption that by promoting women's rights the United States contributes to the democratization of the Arab world.

Confusion About Democracy and Women's Rights

Promotion of women's rights in the Middle East is an easy goal for the United States to announce. It lends itself to resounding rhetorical statements. It can be translated in practice into many concrete, small projects that are not seen as threatening by most Arab regimes and are even welcomed by them as a means to demonstrate their willingness to democratize and modernize. An improvement in the rights of women does not threaten the power of the incumbent authoritarian government in the same way as free elections or a free press would. Except in Saudi Arabia, Arab leaders and opposition political parties alike, including all but the most fundamentalist Islamic organizations, gladly embrace the rhetoric of women's rights. Many governments are even willing to take small concrete steps, such as appointing the occasional woman to a high, visible position, or introducing amendments to divorce or family laws. For the United States and other democracy-promoting countries, women's programs have the added advantage of being relatively cheap and easy to implement—for example, encouraging schooling for girls, financing women's nongovernmental organizations (NGOs), or providing training for women's candidates in countries where women can run for office. The popularity of the women's rights cause and its obvious intrinsic merit have unfortunately generated many facile assumptions and much confusion about the conditions of women in the Middle East and the problems they face; about the relationship between women's rights and democracy; and about what an outside intervenor like the United States can accomplish. This [viewpoint] seeks to clarify some of these issues. It fully accepts the dominant assumptions that the rights of Arab women are not sufficiently protected in the Arab world; that social norms preclude women from fully enjoying even their limited legal rights; that this holds back the entire society; and that the United States should be concerned about the problem and contribute to its solution. It cautions, however, against the assumption that by promoting women's rights the United States contributes to the democratization of the Arab world, and it calls for a clearer separation of programs promoting the rights of women and opportunities for them and those promoting democracy. . . .

The idea that working for women's rights is an integral part of the struggle for democracy is in part tautology and in part simply wrong.

Democracy Predates Women's Suffrage

Support for women's rights in the Arab world is seen in the United States as part of the effort to promote democracy in the region. Yet, the relationship between women's rights and democracy is not simple. The idea that working for women's rights is an integral part of the struggle for democracy is in part a tautology and in part simply wrong. The statement is tautological in the sense that democracy entails equality for all citizens, thus promoting women's rights means promoting democracy. But democracy also entails creating institutions that are accountable to the citizens and [that] curb one another's power through a system of checks and balances. The existence of such institutions does not depend on the rights of women.

These institutions can thrive, and have thrived historically, even when women do not enjoy the same political and civil rights as men. Conversely, states that did not have accountable institutions or a system of checks and balances have recognized the equality of women, historically and even now. Socialist countries in particular emphasized that they promoted the equality of women better than Western countries, while in practice curtailing the political and civil rights of all citizens.

In countries that started developing democratic systems before World War II, democratic political institutions were established over a hundred years before the political rights of women were recognized or even before women's rights emerged as an issue. The United States and Great Britain started developing strong democratic institutions without the benefit of women's suffrage or even of universal male suffrage. Political participation in both countries was originally quite limited. Over the course of the nineteenth century, participation expanded to include the male population—at least the white male population in the United States. Resistance to women's participation continued unabated until 1918 in Great Britain and 1920 in the United States.

> *Recognition of women's rights has not automatically made political systems ... more likely to develop democratic institutions.*

The Battle for Women's Suffrage

The battle for women's suffrage was quite difficult in both countries. Although in retrospect the outcome seems inevitable, it did not appear so at the time. Social values and customs prevented the recognition of equal rights for women, in the same way as they once prevented the recognition of equal rights of racial minorities in the United States. Once women became mobilized, however, the democratic nature of the political system made the outcome inevitable because only a degree of repression untenable in a democratic system could have stopped women from demanding equal rights. Despite widespread social prejudice against women's rights, democratic principles left no other choice. The inclusion of women was part and parcel of democratic consolidation, as was the inclusion of racial minorities in the United States forty years later. The existence of democratic institutions and of a democratic culture and tradition made the inclusion of women and ethnic minorities inevitable in the long run.

After World War II, and in some countries even earlier, the recognition of women's political and civil rights has become routine everywhere, including in countries that did not or do not embrace democracy. What has been historically a dramatic breakthrough toward democratic consolidations has turned almost everywhere into an idea to which almost all countries in the world pay homage, although in reality politics and governance remain a male prerogative almost everywhere. But recognition of women's rights has not automatically made political systems more pluralistic or more likely to develop democratic institutions.

> *There should be no illusion . . . that promoting women's tights will lead to democracy.*

This is quite clear in the Arab world today. Those Arab states that recognize some political rights of citizens—such as being able to elect legislative assemblies—also recognize the political rights of women. Kuwait, which does not recognize political rights for women, is a real anomaly in this regard. What keeps Arab countries from being democratic is not the exclusion of women, but the fact that elected institutions have very little power and impose no effective checks on monarchs who govern as well as rule and on presidents whose power base is in the security forces or a strong party.

Separate Struggles

The struggle for women's rights and the core struggle to achieve democracy—that is, to reduce the excessive and arbitrary power of the executive—must be seen as separate processes in the Arab world today. Progress toward democracy in the Arab world depends on the emergence of countervailing forces and organized groups that the government cannot ignore and that have to be accommodated in the political system. Simply including women in a hollow political process does nothing to create such countervailing forces. This does not mean that the promotion of equal rights for women has to wait until countervailing forces emerge or political institutions that curb the excessive power of the executive are put in place. Certainly, the two battles can be waged simultaneously. There should be no illusion, however, either that promoting women's rights will lead to democracy or that the emergence of institutions of checks and balances will automatically solve the problem of equality for women. . . .

Limited Political Impact

Increased participation by women in political life has hardly any impact on the functioning of political systems. . . . The removal of legal and social barriers that prevent women from enjoying access to education and jobs has a great deal of impact on the personal lives and income-earning capacity of women, and thus on their children. These are not negligible results, and they certainly justify efforts by the United States to promote rights for women as well as their advancement in the society. However, an expectation has developed that women's rights and empowerment in the Arab world will have a more far-reaching impact. As the *Arab Human Development Report 2002* stated, in order to participate fully in the world of the twenty-first century, Arab countries must tackle the deficit of women's empowerment.

Is there reason to believe that the promotion of women's rights, not only in theory but in practice, would have a greater impact in the Arab world than it has had elsewhere? Could promotion of women's rights shake these societies in a much more dramatic way than has been the case elsewhere? Is the extension of women's rights the beginning of a road to profound change in Arab countries, as the rhetoric suggests?

For the vast majority of Arab states, the answer is negative. In most countries, women already enjoy the same political rights, limited as they are, as men. Family status laws are improving slowly in a number of countries; and this process is likely to continue because this is an area where incumbent governments can demonstrate to the world their reforming zeal without undermining their power. Women are also becoming much better educated in most countries, even in the closed societies of the [Persian] Gulf. It is true that social values are changing slowly and that the growth of Islamist movements in many countries is creating new obstacles for women. But in general a gradual process toward improving women's rights is under way.

The political systems of most Arab countries can incorporate such changes in the position of women without difficulty, because their political systems have a degree of flexibility. Although no Arab regimes can be considered democratic, many are semiauthoritarian, combining relatively democratic political institutions and some limited recognition of individual rights and personal freedom with an overly strong executive. Countries such as Egypt, Jordan, or Morocco, for example, have proven adept at maintaining a balance between authoritarianism and limited democratic freedoms, and they can undoubtedly absorb some changes in the position of women without much difficulty. Autocratic but secular countries— Syria, for example, and in the past Iraq—have no problem making concessions to women.

The question of whether the expansion of women's rights would have a different, more far-reaching effect in Arab nations than it had in the rest of the world thus can only be raised in relation to the countries of the Gulf, which are the most closed socially and politically. Even in these countries, however, the present trend is toward slow, cautious social and political reform. Bahrain, Kuwait, Oman, and Qatar are moving hesitantly in that direction, with the governments apparently in full control of the pace of change. Saudi Arabia has been very wary of embarking on any type of reform, social or political, although recent statements suggest that it may decide to follow the example of its neighbors.

In conclusion, there seems to be little reason to expect that improved rights for women in the Middle East would have a more dramatic political impact than similar reforms in the rest of the world. . . .

Confusing the advancement of women and the advancement of democracy is not only incorrect but also dangerous.

The Danger of Focusing on Women's Rights

Advancing women's rights in the Arab world is an important goal, and the United States should continue to pursue it in the name of equity and justice. Improving the position of women might also have a favorable impact on economic growth, children's welfare, and fertility rates, as has been the case in other countries. There should be no illusion, however, that pressuring Arab governments to recognize the rights of women and undertaking projects to improve their lives addresses the most fundamental obstacles to democracy: the unchecked power of strong executives. Promoting democracy and promoting women's rights need to be recognized as tasks that require different approaches.

Whether and how the United States could contribute to the democratic transformation of the Middle East at present is an issue that goes beyond the scope of this [viewpoint]. . . . It is clear, however, that it cannot do so through programs that advance the rights of women and opportunities for them. Confusing the advancement of women and the advancement of democracy is not only incorrect but also dangerous in the atmosphere of deep distrust of the United States that already exists in the Middle East. Conflating democracy and the advancement of women encourages liberal Arabs, who are already doubtful about the U.S. commitment to democracy, to become even more skeptical—the United States has chosen to teach girls to read instead of confronting autocratic governments. Conservative Arabs, who already tend to interpret the moral degeneration (in their eyes) of the West to be a result of democracy, worry even more when U.S. officials talk about democracy and trying to change the position of women in their societies. The identification of democracy and women's rights leads to sinister interpretations and unintended consequences in the Arab world. There is great need for the U.S. government not only to rethink the nexus of democracy and the promotion of women, but also to become more sensitive to the great gap that separates what U.S. officials say and what different Arab constituencies hear.

Organizations to Contact

**America-Mideast Educational and
Training Services (AMIDEAST)**
1730 M St. NW, Ste. 1100, Washington, DC   20036-4505
(202) 776-9600 • fax: (202) 776-7000
e-mail: inquiries@amideast.org
Web site: www.amideast.org

AMIDEAST promotes understanding and cooperation between Americans and the people of the Middle East and North
Africa through education and development programs. It publishes a number of books for all age groups, including *Islam:
A Primer*.

American Enterprise Institute (AEI)
1150 Seventeenth St. NW, Washington, DC   20036
(202) 862-5800 • fax: (202) 862-7177
Web site: www.aei.org

The American Enterprise Institute for Public Policy Research
is a scholarly research institute that is dedicated to preserving
limited government, private enterprise, and a strong foreign
policy and national defense. It publishes books, including
*Democratic Realism: An American Foreign Policy for a Unipolar
World* and *The Islamic Paradox: Shiite Clerics, Sunni Fundamentalists, and the Coming of Arab Democracy*; and the bimonthly magazine *American Enterprise*.

**Arab World and Islamic Resources and
School Services (AWAIR)**
2137 Rose St., Berkeley, CA   94709
(510) 704-0517
e-mail: awair@igc.apc.org
Web site: www.telegraphave.com/gui/awairproductinfo.html

AWAIR provides materials and services for educators teaching about Arabs and Islam for precollege-level educators. It publishes many books and videos, including *The Arab World Notebook*, *Middle Eastern Muslim Women Speak*, and *Islam*.

The Brookings Institution
1775 Massachusetts Ave. NW, Washington, DC 20036
(202) 797-6000 • fax: (202) 797-6004
e-mail: brookinfo@brook.edu
Web site: www.brookings.org

The institution, founded in 1927, is a think tank that conducts research and education in foreign policy, economics, government, and the social sciences. In 2001 it began America's Response to Terrorism, a project that provides briefings and analysis to the public and which is featured on the center's Web site. It publishes the quarterly *Brookings Review*, periodic *Policy Briefs*, and books, including titles on the Middle East such as *Crescent of Crisis* and *Iran, Islam, and Democracy*.

Cato Institute
1000 Massachusetts Ave. NW, Washington, DC 2001-5403
(202) 842-0200 • fax: (202) 842-3490
e-mail: cato@cato.org
Web site: www.cato.org

The institute is a nonpartisan public policy research foundation dedicated to limiting the role of government and protecting individual liberties. It publishes the quarterly magazine *Regulation*, the bimonthly *Cato Policy Report*, and numerous policy papers and articles.

Council on Foreign Relations
58 E. Sixty-eighth St., New York, NY 10021
(212) 434-9400 • fax: (212) 434-9800
e-mail: communications@cfr.org
Web site: www.cfr.org

The council researches the international aspects of American economic and political policies. Its journal *Foreign Affairs*, published five times a year, provides analysis on global conflicts. Publications include "Threats to Democracy: Prevention and Response" and various articles. A video recording of the proceedings of a December 2005 conference, called *Democracy in the Arab World—Why and How,* can be viewed on its Web site.

International Institute of Islamic Thought (IIIT)
PO Box 669, Herndon, VA   20172
(703) 471-1133 • fax: (703) 471-3922
e-mail: iiit@iiit.org
Web site: www.iiit.org

This nonprofit academic research facility promotes and coordinates research and related activities in Islamic philosophy, the humanities, and social sciences. It publishes numerous books in both Arabic and English as well as the quarterly *American Journal of Islamic Social Science* and the *Muslim World Book Review.*

Islamic Supreme Council of America (ISCA)
1400 Sixteenth St. NW, Rm. B-112, Washington, DC   20036
(202) 939-3400 • fax: (202) 939-3410
e-mail: staff@islamicsupremecouncil.org
Web site: www.islamicsupremecouncil.org

The ISCA is a nongovernmental religious organization that promotes Islam in America both by providing practical solutions to American Muslims in integrating Islamic teachings with American culture and by teaching non-Muslims that Islam is a religion of moderation, peace, and tolerance. It strongly condemns Islamic extremists and all forms of terrorism. Its Web site includes statements, commentaries, and reports on terrorism, including *Osama bin Laden: A Legend Gone Wrong* and *Jihad: A Misunderstood Concept from Islam.*

Middle East Media Research Institute (MEMRI)
PO Box 27837, Washington, DC   20038-7837
(202) 955-9070 • fax: (202) 955-9077

e-mail: memri@erols.com
Web site: www.memri.org

MEMRI translates and disseminates articles and commentaries from Middle East media sources and provides original research and analysis on the region. Its Jihad and Terrorism Studies Project monitors radical Islamist groups and individuals and their reactions to acts of terrorism around the world.

Middle East Policy Council
1730 M St. NW, Ste. 512, Washington, DC 20036
(202) 296-6767 • fax: (202) 296-5791
e-mail: info@mepc.org
Web site: www.mepc.org

The purpose of this nonprofit organization is to contribute to an understanding of current issues in U.S. relations with countries of the Middle East. It publishes the quarterly journal *Middle East Policy* as well as special reports and books.

Middle East Studies Association
University of Arizona, Tucson, AZ 85721
(520) 621-5850 • fax: (520) 626-9095
e-mail: mesana@u.arizona.edu
Web site: http://w3fp.arizona.edu/mesassoc

This professional academic association of scholars on the Middle East focuses particularly on the rise of Islam. It publishes the quarterly *International Journal of Middle East Studies* and runs a project for the evaluation of textbooks for coverage of the Middle East.

The National Endowment for Democracy (NED)
1101 Fifteenth St. NW, Ste. 700, Washington, DC 20005
(202) 293-9072 • fax: (202) 223-6042
e-mail: info@ned.org

NED is a private nonprofit organization created in 1983 to strengthen democratic institutions around the world through nongovernmental efforts. It publishes the bimonthly periodical *Journal of Democracy*.

United Association for Studies and Research
PO Box 1210, Annandale, VA   22003-1210
(703) 750-9011 • fax: (703) 750-9010
e-mail: uasr@aol.com
Web site: www.uasr4islam.com

This nonprofit organization examines the causes of conflict in the Middle East and North Africa, the political trends that shape the region's future, and the relationship of the region to more technologically advanced nations. It publishes *Islam Under Siege* and *The Middle East: Politics and Development*, two series of occasional papers on current topics.

United Nations Development Programme (UNDP)
One United Nations Plaza, New York, NY   10017
(212) 906-5317
Web site: www.undp.org

The United Nations was established in 1945 to, among other things, help nations cooperate in solving international economic, social, cultural, and humanitarian problems. The UNDP engages in global advocacy and analysis to generate knowledge about—and develop policies to aid—developing nations. UNDP's primary areas of interest are democratic governance, poverty reduction, environmental protection, sustainable energy, gender issues, HIV/AIDS, information and communication technology, and crisis prevention and recovery. Numerous reports and fact sheets on these topics are available on the UNDP Web site.

Washington Institute for Near East Policy
1828 L St. NW, Washington, DC   20036
(202) 452-0650 • fax: (202) 223-5364
e-mail: info@washingtoninstitute.org
Web site: www.washingtoninstitute.org

The institute is an independent nonprofit research organization that provides information and analysis on the Middle East and U.S. policy in the region. It publishes numerous books, periodic monographs, and reports on regional politics, security, and economics, including *Hezbollah's Vision of the West, Hamas: The Fundamentalist Challenge to the PLO, Democracy and Arab Political Culture,* and *Democracy in the Middle East: Defining the Challenge.*

Women's Alliance for Democracy in Iraq (WAFDI)
e-mail: sarbaghsalih@cs.com
Web site: www.wafdi.org

WAFDI is an international nonpartisan and not-for-profit women's rights organization dedicated to a free and democratic Iraq with full and equal individual rights for women. The organization is committed to the advancement and empowerment of women in all areas of society, including but not limited to family, economics, education, health, arts, literature, sports, and politics.

Bibliography

Books

Edwin Black   *Banking on Baghdad: Inside Iraq's 7,000-Year History of War, Profit, and Conflict.* New York: Wiley, 2004.

Edmund Bourke and David N. Yaghoubi, eds.   *Struggle and Survival in the Modern Middle East.* Berkeley and Los Angeles: University of California Press, 2006.

Thomas Carothers and Marina Ottaway, eds.   *Uncharted Journey: Promoting Democracy in the Middle East.* Washington, DC: Brookings Institution, 2005.

William Crotty, ed.   *Democratic Development and Political Terrorism: The Global Perspective.* Boston: Northeastern University Press, 2005.

Alex Danchev and John MacMillan, eds.   *The Iraq War and Democratic Politics.* London: Routledge, 2005.

Larry Diamond   *Squandered Victory: The American Occupation and the Bungled Effort to Bring Democracy to Iraq.* New York: Times Books/Henry Holt, 2005.

Larry Diamond, Marc F. Plattner, and Daniel Brumberg, eds.   *Islam and Democracy in the Middle East.* Baltimore: Johns Hopkins University Press, 2003.

Larry Diamond,   *World Religions and Democracy.* Balti-
Marc F. Plattner,   more: Johns Hopkins University
and Philip J.   Press, 2005.
Costopoulos, eds.

Freedom House   *Freedom in the Middle East and
                    North Africa: A* Freedom in the
                    World *Special Edition.* Lanham, MD:
                    Rowman and Littlefield, 2005.

Graham E. Fuller   *The Future of Political Islam.* New
                    York: Palgrave Macmillan, 2004.

James L. Gelvin   *The Modern Middle East.* New York:
                    Oxford University Press, 2005.

Jude Howell and   *Gender and Civil Society: Transcend-
Diane Mulligan,   ing Boundaries.* New York: Routledge,
eds.   2005.

Mehran Kamrava   *The Modern Middle East: A Political
                    History Since the First World War.*
                    Berkeley and Los Angeles: University
                    of California Press, 2005.

Rashid Khalid   *Resurrecting Empire: Western Foot-
                    prints and America's Perilous Path in
                    the Middle East.* Boston: Beacon,
                    2004.

Jean Said Makdisi   *Teta, Mother and Me: An Arab
                    Woman's Memoir.* London: Saqi,
                    2005.

Roger Owen   *State, Power and Politics in the Mak-
                    ing of the Modern Middle East.* New
                    York: Routledge, 2004.

Barry M. Rubin — *The Long War for Freedom: The Arab Struggle for Democracy in the Middle East.* Hoboken, NJ: Wiley, 2006.

William A. Rugh — *American Encounters with Arabs: The "Soft Power" of U.S. Public Diplomacy in the Middle East.* Westport, CT: Praeger Security International, 2006.

Amin Saikal and Albrecht Schnabel, eds. — *Democratization in the Middle East: Experiences, Struggles, Challenges.* New York: United Nations University Press, 2003.

Natan Sharansky — *The Case for Democracy: The Power of Freedom to Overcome Tyranny and Terror.* Cambridge, MA: Perseus, 2004.

Periodicals

Imad-ad-Dean Ahmad — "Reconciling Secular Government with Democracy," paper delivered at the CSID Sixth Annual Conference, Democracy and Development: Challenges for the Islamic World, Washington, DC, April 22–23, 2005.

Patrick Basham — "Can Iraq Be Democratic?" *Policy Analysis,* January 5, 2004.

Edwin Black — "Given Its History, Can We Succeed in Iraq?" *History News Network,* December 27, 2004.

John Bunzl, ed.   *Islam, Judaism, and the Political Role of Religions in the Middle East.* Gainesville: University Press of Florida, 2004.

Joan Chittister   "What the World Told Karen Hughes," *National Catholic Reporter,* October 14, 2005.

Adeed Dawisha   "Iraq: Setbacks, Advances and Prospects," *Journal of Democracy,* January, 2004.

Adeed Dawisha   "The Prospects for Democracy in Iraq," *Third World Quarterly,* July/ August 2005.

Todd Frantom   "Building Democracy in Iraq," *All Hands,* May 2005.

Jamie Glazov   "Symposium: The War for the Soul of Iraq," *FrontPageMagazine.com,* December 2, 2005. www.frontpagemaga zine.com.

Michael Ignatieff   "Who Are Americans to Think That Freedom Is Theirs to Spread?" *New York Times Magazine,* June 26, 2005.

Marisa Katz   "Democratease—Rhetoric v. Reality," *New Republic,* June 6, 2005.

Joshua Moravchik   "Among Arab Reformers," *Commentary,* September 2005.

Sheikha Mozah   "Give Arab Women Their Due," *Peninsula,* March 4, 2006.

Vali Nasr   "The Rise of Muslim Democracy," *Journal of Democracy*, April 2005.

Marina S. Ottaway   "Keep the Faith—Islamists and Democracy," *New Republic*, June 6, 2005.

Marina S. Ottaway et al.   "Democracy: Rising Tide or Mirage?" *Middle East Policy*, Summer 2005.

Carla Power and Reem Haddad   "Look Who's Talking: What's the Best Way to Spread Democracy in the Middle East? Maybe Through Homegrown Reality and Talk TV Shows," *Newsweek International*, August 8, 2005.

Alan Richards   "Democracy in the Arab Region: Getting There from Here," *Middle East Policy*, Summer 2005.

Susan Sachs   "Are Islam and Democracy Compatible? Democracy Is Taking Hold in Some Countries; in Others, Especially in the Middle East, the Prospects Are Unclear," *New York Times Upfront*, December 13, 2004.

Roger Scruton   "Limits to Democracy," *New Criterion*, January 2006.

Lance Selfa   "Democratic Illusions," *International Socialist Review*, May/June, 2005.

Amir Taheri   "The Future of US Foreign Policy: A Debate Rages in Washington," *Asharq Alawsat*, December 9, 2005. www.asharqalawsat.com/english/.

United Nations
Development
Programme

"Towards Freedom in the Arab World," Arab Human Development Report, 2004.

Wall Street Journal

"Democracy Angst: What's the Alternative to Promoting Democracy in the Middle East?" editorial, February 27, 2006.

Washington Post

"The Case for Democracy," editorial, March 5, 2006.

George F. Will

"Can We Make Iraq Democratic?" *City Journal*, Winter 2004.

Mona Yacoubian

"Promoting Middle East Democracy II: Arab Initiatives," United States Institute of Peace, 2005.

Mai Yamani

"Democratic Façade (Democracy and Muslim Law in Saudi Arabia)," *World Today*, February 2005.

Dov S. Zakheim

"Blending Democracy: The Generational Project in the Middle East," *National Interest*, Fall 2005.

Index